Life As We *Don't* Know It

The mind-blowing fact of how your thoughts become your reality.

Mahi Amin

Life As We Don't Know It
Copyright © 2021 Mahi Amin
First published in 2021

Print: 978-1-76124-001-0
E-book: 978-1-76124-002-7
Hardback: 978-1-76124-000-3

All rights reserved. No part of this book may be reproduced, stored in a retrieval system, or transmitted by any means (electronic, mechanical, photocopying, recording, or otherwise) without written permission from the author.

Because of the dynamic nature of the Internet, any web addresses or links contained in this book may have changed since publication and may no longer be valid. The information in this book is based on the author's experiences and opinions. The views expressed in this book are solely those of the author and do not necessarily reflect the views of the publisher; the publisher hereby disclaims any responsibility for them.

The author of this book does not dispense any form of medical, legal, financial, or technical advice either directly or indirectly. The intent of the author is solely to provide information of a general nature to help you in your quest for personal development and growth. In the event you use any of the information in this book, the author and the publisher assume no responsibility for your actions. If any form of expert assistance is required, the services of a competent professional should be sought.

Publishing information
Publishing, design, and production facilitated by Passionpreneur Publishing, A division of Passionpreneur Organization Pty Ltd, ABN: 48640637529

www.PassionpreneurPublishing.com
Melbourne, VIC | Australia

TABLE OF CONTENTS

Disclaimer	v
Testimonials	vii
Dedication	xi
Acknowledgments	xiii

Part I

Introduction	3

Part II

What My Childhood Was Like	15
What My Adulthood Looks Like	25

Part III

The Flight Attendant Phase	45
The Environment	55
Relationship/Situationship	71

Part IV

Are You "Smart Enough"?   97

You Are Feeling Your Thoughts   111

E-motion   131

Conclusion & Closure   145

About the Author   189

DISCLAIMER

This is a work of creative non-fiction. All of the events in this book are true to the best of the author's memory. Some names and identifying features have been changed to protect the identity of certain parties. The author in no way represents any company, corporation, or brand, mentioned herein. The views expressed in this book are solely those of the author.

TESTIMONIALS

I first met Mahi when introduced to her by a friend whom I play volleyball with on a beach here in Dubai. She had the biggest smile and most infectious energy, which was both compelling and inviting. We sat and talked on the beach, and unlike so many of us, who speak to respond, she was genuinely interested in who I was and what I had to say. She asked many skillful questions and listened intently to the replies and then offered very proficient observations. Since that day, we have become good friends, and her inquisitive nature and thirst for learning have never abated, and hence her career as a life coach is a natural fit. She is both wise and informed, and when engaged, will help you to become your most refined version. Mahi is a breath of fresh air, and the world is a far better place with her in it.

Darren Jon Timms. Counseling psychologist,
Transformation coach and the author of the Amazon
number 1 bestseller "The Journey Back To Self" –
A Roadmap of Rediscovery.

Mahi Amin...
Well, I met her through the sport.

I was her boxing coach, and I was surprised by the energy she has. I was wondering what type of batteries she's using to be so positive and full of good vibes. Training by training, apart from her amazing skills and passion for sports, I've noticed that waves of positive thoughts that are coming from her. There were days I wasn't in the mood and tried to hide it, but after training with her, my batteries were charged with positive energy. Yes, I know it should be the opposite, it simply happened this way sometimes. Later on, I've noticed that I like the days I will meet her, firstly because she does great boxing, and secondly because I was really enjoying being in her company and talking honestly about life with her while having a break in between sets. Definitely a person who can listen and give good advice...

Milos Teofilovic, Fitness Trainer and
former French Boxing champion.

Energetic. Transformative. UPLIFTING! Mahi is simply a ball of energy! She is a fantastic life coach, great fun to talk to, and has an impressive ability to get to the root of a problem. Her passion for growth and empathetic, caring nature makes her a truly unique and inspiring coach. The time I spend with Mahi is always fun, relaxed, and extremely informative. I truly admire her love for coaching and it is evident in her liveliness, deep presence, and how she offers her experience freely. Hire Mahi! She is an amazing coach and friend.

Noura Al Abbasi,
Transformation Coach

Mahi is a very open-hearted, fun, and energetic coach. She has a non-judgmental and compassionate approach with her clients. I instantly felt at ease as she coached me through some sensitive topics. She also encourages me to play and just go with it without being too attached to any specific outcome.

Highly recommended.

Beth Hutchinson, Grief Recovery Coach
and Founder of Peaceful Life Hub.

If by way of introduction or a chance meeting you are fortunate enough that Mahi Amin has entered your life, take this as a blessing, because the opportunity to know her will change your life in some way. As a person, Mahi is a shining example of everything we all strive to be – her spirit fills any room she enters and she possess an alluring quality that draws people to her. Positivity, laughs, and good energy is what you will get when you're around Mahi Amin. Mahi has always radiated like this, so it's no surprise that she found her calling in helping others achieve their best selves.

As a coach, Mahi invests all her attention to be your advocate. As someone that struggles with the concept of letting go, I was surprised that Mahi was able to personalize her teachings in a way that I would respond to. Mahi quickly helped me break through emotional blockages that I was holding onto that prevented my life from moving forward. Shortly after my first session with Mahi my life began to feel easier and good things began coming into my life effortlessly after I was stuck in a rut. I am so grateful Mahi took the time to share this knowledge with me and raise my consciousness, as it will positively impact the rest of my life.

Robert Anthony – Writer, micro-influencer
@FlexAroundtheWorld (Instagram / Podcast)

DEDICATION

This book is based on real stories of real people. I do know these people and/or what they shared from their own life experiences.

Usually it goes like this: you pick up a book, flip through it, reach the dedication part, and find that once again, the author has dedicated the book to someone else, and not you.

Not this time. We most likely haven't met yet. Maybe we never will. I don't know. What I do know is that the Universe is connecting us on a higher level than just in the physical plane and that you're going to feel this connection throughout your reading journey.

And *that* is the reason why I dedicate this book to you.

May you find, in this sharing, a way of clarity, inner peace, and the wisdom to self-acceptance.

ACKNOWLEDGMENTS

I would like to acknowledge each and every one who helped and supported me throughout my journey of writing this book and bringing it to the light of day, including all my fellow coaches, friends, family members, and very much the publishing team for their effort and patience.

Special thanks to my beautiful brother, Marwan Amin, who supported me at all times and has been like a strong backbone for me.

To my great friends/coaches, Noura Al Abbasi and Darren Timms, who helped and guided me so I could keep my sanity and balance in place when I needed it most.

To my beautiful friends, Noha Shaarawy and Nihal El Gendy, who are always by my side whenever I need them.

To my amazing trainer, Robert Simic, who has provided me with so many learnings and so much knowledge that I have been exposed to. To Corinna Klose, who had the patience and wisdom to help and advise me whenever needed.

To my coach Luke, who has guided and helped me when I needed my creativity mode back on.

And last but not least to Subhashini Nandakumar, who helped in my healing process during my training and introduced me to the publishing institution once she heard I was in the process of writing my book.

Part I

1

INTRODUCTION

For as long as I can remember, I've always been a good storyteller (as I go into every single detail of the story). But being a writer! Oh boy… that is a different ballgame altogether.

The feeling of being judged in public is definitely not easy, I would say. But here I am, doing a scary thing. Right?

My decision to write about my life experience before my 30th birthday is an early gift to myself. I am, in addition, hoping you find some benefit in it for yourself, one way or another.

Why do I think this would benefit you?

Simply because I believe that we are all learning from and with each other, and guiding and walking one another through our paths. I was raised in an Arabic culture (Egypt), and then moved to the UAE. My life in both these places — their culture, their social mores, their dos and don'ts had a great impact on me.

My job as a flight attendant, too, definitely left its mark on who I am. But let's go back to early life first, shall we?

I've been that kid who asks loads of questions — why this and how that — is kind of a rebel, disagrees on things She isn't really convinced about.

The rigidity of my culture didn't really fancy a woman with a rebellious personality, hence I faced so many challenges in this 'manly' society. The struggle was really hard. How could I make society not only hear the words I was speaking, but actually listen to me? You get the difference? In addition to the judgment of being a girl, I was also a disobedient child! It started with the family at home (which you will read about in greater detail as you go through the book), neighbors, teachers at school, friends, and, as I mentioned before, society in general.

Too many rules and laws would chain me and define how I grew up.

I'm certain that this happens in so many other cultures and not only the Middle East. However, I am talking about what *I* experienced, what *my* attitude was towards it, how *I* dealt with it in the past, and how *I* am dealing with it now.

I was a smart kid, super hyper, and loved to dance. I still love to dance, and I'm also still super hyper. I remember I wanted to become a ballet dancer. I would always walk on my toes and wear my mom's, or any of her friend's, heels and would try walking on my toes while wearing them.

Nothing moved my parents. They still did not send me to a ballet school – they were possibly waiting for me to walk on the wall or something!

I also liked to write in my diaries about my feelings as I was growing up, who my crush was, what happened that day, and all the other things young girls write about in their diaries. Much to the dismay of my dear mother, I loved to listen to music, sing, and help us all, even act! I would talk to myself and create my favorite character of the day. I even wanted to travel the world and become a flight attendant. Well, as you know now, that part got done. Just waiting for the acting part, though!

Despite being considered a rebel, I was a very sensitive child who loved life and was always seeking more, just like most kids, I guess.

I had so many friends, not all of them were Arabs. My English back then wasn't that great, even though my mom (bless her) worked very hard to teach me the basics. One of the most important basics is the difference between "P and B" as P is not a recognizable letter in the Arabic alphabet. Also, to improve my language, I would ask my friends to speak in English with me, so I could listen to their pronunciation and learn. And *this* is how I learned to speak English really. When I was 19, working with native English speakers helped me improve my language. I loved it enough to have adopted it as my chosen language and that was enough to make me keep learning it passionately.

Did I startle you by sharing that I was working at 19? Well, I actually started working at 18!

The Arabic culture did not look very kindly on girls working, especially while studying, back in the day. Only a little has changed today. I am, however, not very good with doing and following what doesn't make sense to me. I wanted to be independent and have my own money. I was, in fact, the only one then among all my Arab friends to work. I thought I was doing pretty good for myself, so far.

I created my own personality from a very young age and I made sure I created a strong one, and the older I get, the more I'm aware of what a strong personality is, what the differences are between my personality and my beliefs – old and new – and how that affects me as a human being raised in a culture of huge amount of pride, ego, and rigidity.

What I learned is that ownership, money orientation, and stubbornness exist in the majority of us and create limiting and fearful beliefs about ourselves and the world that we live in.

Living abroad alone was challenging. My friends back home in their 30s, 40s, or even 50s struggle to do it, especially when they have responsibilities and commitments. Travelling alone is still a brand-new idea in our culture. I feel so blessed and grateful to have the luxury of doing all that by myself. Who would believe I could do that, when I was allowed to go out only once a month during my high school? I was not even allowed to date someone because of my dad, as he is a very strict, closed-minded, micro-controlling man who's been influnced by society and traditions that made him very conscious of social rules over anything else. So, I would hide pretty much everything from him. I would tell my mom and brother about my boyfriend back then, because I knew I wasn't doing anything wrong. We used to meet infrequently, thanks to all my studies (which, like most of us, I neither liked much nor thought were very useful). However, my mother had certain rules which if I followed I could meet him. Those days, I could only meet my boyfriend after a lesson for around an hour or so.

And it wasn't just my boyfriend. The restrictions were such that my friends could not visit me, and vice-versa.

I could never imagine back then that my life would turn out the way it did. Or perhaps because I was wishing deep inside to turn my life to something I love and because my passion to change was so strong, that's why it changed.

I'll tell you one thing though, Once I started earning my own money and told my parents I wanted to be independent and wouldn't want to ask them for anything, pretty much everything changed from my mom's side. Of course, my dad never liked the idea of me working.

I ended up graduating with an 'OK' degree, which was kind of expected, as I was doing something that I didn't even like. I couldn't join the famous acting academy that I wanted to, because I had a lisp back then that I got rid of overtime. I was sent to a private academy to study IT (Information Technology System)! Like really? Making me do more things of what I don't like! I only chose that academy as it didn't have too much emphasis on attendance. This way, at least, I could work through the year and just attend the mid-term and final exams!

My first job was at a life insurance company. That was quite serious. The company provided for us a very useful course, which I remember nothing about "consciously", but I remember back then it was intense, especially as it was about human physiology and how to deal with their assets when they died!

I was supposed to go convince some clients – young me, just 18 years of age, and this was my first job ever – that if they took the insurance, when they died, their money would go to their family and ensure their comfort and safety. What if this person didn't really fancy their family much? What was I really telling this person? To add to that, in our culture we believe it is bad luck to talk about death in any way. Life insurance was not an easy business in my culture back then, as popular belief was that it was *haram* (forbidden). Life insurance may have become more popular in recent times, but it doesn't make it any less forbidden. It took nearly two months for me to resign. Apart from the workload, my manager was flirting with me and if I hadn't left the office when he started flirting, he would have sexually harassed me one day.

After that, I worked as a waitress in one of the restaurants for a couple of months. I had to leave to write my exams. Just as well – the manager didn't really like me anyway. He felt threatened by me because the owner really liked me. She was giving me special treatment because she liked the fact that I was studying while working! It might sound normal to you; you might even think: what was so great about working while studying? It is not a usual thing, especially for a girl back home. At least it wasn't back then.

Then I became an assistant teacher. I had challenges from dealing with different mentalities and cultures. That's when I learnt that not all people like to see someone else successful, especially in their field. They consider that as a threat to their role. It was one of the most beautiful experiences I have had. I learned a lot and I know for sure that I wouldn't have moved forward if I didn't have this experience.

What followed was the job of an English teacher. This was an on-off assignment that kept changing its shape. I would work as an English teacher, then as a (not professional) translator at an export-import company. My English was becoming good enough to attend meetings and translate what was happening!

After that, I took the job of a receptionist at a boutique hotel. I have to say, that is my third favorite job ever! I did have the same challenges when I was assistant teacher – of people being threatened by someone successful or good at what they do – but it was on a deeper level. I had one of my most long-lasting lessons about backstabbing and deceiving from one of the best teachers I have met in my work life – my colleague who did the same work I did. By then, I knew I had entered the corporate life.

There was another job I did in public relations (PR) in a petroleum services company. I really liked that one as well.

And all of these, I had experienced between the ages of 18-23!

My second favorite is, of course, being a flight attendant, which is where I have spent most of my 20s – travelling the world and experiencing things I could not even imagine.

At some point, between flights, I started to think about my purpose and passion in this life, so I started working on my career as a Transformation Coach. This is my favorite along with writing so far! Why? because I do not consider it a "job". It is something that fulfills my soul, emotions, mind, and body.

That has been my life, so far. From being denied things that seem so normal to carving my own path.

So, if anyone tells you that you can't have everything you want, stop them right there and tell them, "Thanks for sharing, but I CAN have everything I want." How much you want it and what you are doing to get it is what matters the most. Don't let anyone limit you from dreaming! Instead, become your own unlimited potential and design your own dreams.

Part II

2

WHAT MY CHILDHOOD WAS LIKE

I was born to a middle-class family. We lived in (what used to be) a fancy area in Cairo, called Maadi. I don't remember her, but I've been told we used to have a lady who helped my mom in the house and who my dad cheated on my mom with. Since then, we had no more ladies helping my mom in the house. We also had a driver. We had two apartments – the one we lived in and another one that was just hanging there, for some reason. My father had a built-in sound system and speakers in an L-shaped design around our living room – which was quite cool and unique in the 80s. My mother used to design my dresses, especially for my birthdays. I recall the love and effort she would put in to throw a party for my birthday. She would bake my cake and pizzas, decorate the whole house and invite all my friends and neighbors. She would dance all night with the other moms, then the next day she would start to clean the house all by herself! She would stand on a chair and clean each and every single crystal in all the chandeliers around the house. She was my hero when I was little and I've always wanted to be pretty and strong like her.

My mom is from Aswan, one of the most beautiful places in Egypt when it comes to culture, authenticity, and history. She had always dreamt of living in the big city of Cairo, so she moved there to study archaeology in Cairo University, which was one of, if not the biggest universities in the Middle East back then. But after graduation, she went back to Aswan as in the Arabic culture women can't live alone and leave their parents' house until marriage. She was so pretty then. She is still gorgeous, of course (in case if she reads the book. I am just kidding, of course). She has fair skin, an hourglass body, and dark blonde curly hair – all unusual features for Egyptian women, especially from the south, and that made her look special and exotic for locals.

Even as a kid, I've seen her love for dressing up – she would let some of the hair right at her hair-line show just a little bit from underneath the veil, and she would style herself in somewhat high heels with blazers and a pair of trousers. I remember when she used to come and visit me at school, everyone, starting from teachers to kids, would whisper to each other that my mom was there. As soon as she would leave, I would get so many compliments about her beauty and elegance.

Once back to Aswan, mom received a lot of proposals for marriage – she was so beautiful and well educated. She refused so many proposals from doctors, engineers, lawyers, etc. just because they were not living in the city! She accepted the one sent by my dad, who proposed through her cousin. He lived in Cairo and as I've been told, he said that he had a college degree – just so he could marry my mom. Truth is, he didn't even finish high school.

My dad is from Sohag. It's a city on the west bank of the Nile in Egypt. He finished what he could at school, then moved to Cairo in his early days and started a few businesses. He is a smart entrepreneur who creates ideas and finds ways to create new businesses. For instance, he currently owns a couple of interior home finishing shops. I'm told he was quite charming when he was a young man. I don't know too much about what his life was like or who he was, as we were never really close. When he met mom, he owned a shop for car accessories and was financially comfortable, but there wasn't a love story between them, and because of the education gap, they were never compatible and that created an unhealthy relationship between the two of them. They lived together in Cairo after marriage. Till she gave birth to a gorgeous child – me! My mom was working as a tour guide. She liked what she was doing, but she had to leave her job to take care of me. It was definitely a big sacrifice. When I grew up a little, she started working as an English teacher at one of the biggest schools in the area back then. This is where I went to school for some time. When I was 4 years of age, I got a beautiful brother who I'm grateful for. Eventually, mom started working as an archaeologist. Slowly, things started to be different. My dad sold the shop as well as the other apartment and started working for a petroleum company as a driver – which we were never proud of, as society frames that as a less respectful job. That created even more of a gap between them. I guess my mom never loved my dad and vice versa. I know there was cheating involved and physical and verbal abuse, loud voices, and fighting almost every day. It became absolutely normal for me to see them fighting and shouting.

Thanks to the toxic atmosphere my brother and I were being raised in, it was no wonder I was biting almost everything I saw. Even a dog! Yes, I have been told that I bitten a dog – not the other way around! I would bite my neighbor's new-born baby's little finger. I mean if I did anything wrong my mom would bite or hit *me*. How was any other behavior expected from me? We learn everything from our parents or caregivers, right?

When the chick I had died, my response as grief and resentment was stepping on my neighbor's chicks – two or maybe more – till a second later they were squeezed.

All this sounds so bad, right? Well, that was the outcome from all the anger, violence, and abuse I witnessed as a child.

As a child, I was very stubborn and the older I got, the more questions I asked. I never liked being told what to do, so I would get shouted at or even get beaten. This was in addition to the sexual abuse that I experienced when I was little – in different ways, from different people and different events. I remember, once I was playing hide and seek with all my neighbors. The boy who was seeking us all found me and told me to look away because he was doing something behind me. I didn't even know what it was that he was doing – I was between the ages of seven and eight. I thought that he just wanted to wee. Now, of course, I know it wasn't that. Sexual abuse was both from direct relatives and even strangers. Yes, that's right, the majority of women in the world have been sexually abused, so I'm not that special in this. It is almost rare to see a woman who has not been sexually or, at the very least, physically or verbally abused. If you know one, well, *that* is special. Most women don't share these things with anybody – not even with their family – out of fear or being judged. Even I didn't speak about it until I became 17 or 18 years of age.

Despite all this, I was a very cheerful child. I felt free once I was with my friends, felt that I could express myself freely and laugh out loud and no one would tell me to lower my voice. I could cross my legs while sitting down and no one would tell me to sit up properly. It was small things that kept me cheery, but it was as soon as I stepped out of my home, because the environment there was very toxic in so many ways.

It wasn't just that. I had to leave the pre- and primary school I liked, and the friends I made, and go to a wholly different level of primary school – "government school". The level of friends and society here was not the same. One teacher was sexually abusing me; another one would take me out of the class and put me in time-out. He was the math teacher and his daughter was in the same class as I. I really liked math back then. One day, he gave the class a math challenge and I ended up solving it. He and the other teacher, who one day physically abused me in another event, told me, "The next time, don't answer anything even if you know it." The math teacher shouted at me, saying that his daughter was crying because of me, that she was the one supposed to answer not me! At that time, I felt very scared, sad, and unworthy of expressing myself or standing out!

Of course, *now* I finally know that all of what they did, was coming from ignorance, anger, and resentment – negative emotions that had nothing to do with me – and that teacher was just trying to protect his own daughter's emotions.

Why did I attract all this into my life? Probably to learn from it all and know what feels wrong and what feels right, know what kindness is and how powerful it is, and know what forgiveness is and how powerful it is to forgive, especially when you don't have to. There could be so many lessons learnt here – you can choose your own, rather than staying in resentment and anger. You choose which one would make you feel better.

These weren't the only events that made my childhood what it was. One day, my parents got divorced and my mom went back to her family leaving my brother and me with my dad – that was the only way my dad would agree to the divorce. I remember, after the divorce my dad took my brother and I to my uncle's house so we could play with our cousins. Suddenly, out of nowhere, my uncle started shouting at me and telling me, "Don't you dare become like your mom. If you ever become like her, I will burn you with this cigarette." He had one in his hand, and voilà, he put out the cigarette on my arm. I remember my little body crumbling in a corner on the floor next to the door. I remember crying out and screaming in extreme fear and pain. My dad pulled him away after he did that. Well, too late, buddy. However, I can see now that this man, my uncle, was just angry and full of fear and it had nothing to do with me. Back then, of course, I hated him and never wanted to visit his house again.

I also remember during that time, I had to go to school, and the building security had to drop me there on his bike – there was no bus to pick me up and drop me like my other school, and my dad was asleep. I was seven or eight years of age back then. Once I reached my class, one of my classmates told me that the teacher was off work that day. So, I decided to go back home by myself. The school wasn't too far from my house, so I walked it back. I arrived home and was afraid to ring the bell, even though I didn't do anything wrong. But, as I said, everything I did seemed wrong to my dad. Just as I had expected, my dad got really angry at me for leaving the school, and he started shouting at me asking, "Did you run away from your school?" I did not even know what that even meant at that time, and before I could understand what he was saying, straight away I received an amazingly strong slap on my tiny little face that reached my ears. I started to hear some whistling in my ears, mixed with the voice of my dad still shouting. I felt some warm water flowing out from my ear – that was my ear bleeding. My dad ran – no, not to the hospital but to the phone to ring my mom and use my crying. He made me tell her that he hit me and my ear was bleeding, and that I wanted her to come back!

Now, of course, I look at the situation and I completely understand that this was his level of awareness and understanding to protect his child, and the fear of losing control over us because of my mom's absence. But, back then, I hated him for what seems like forever because of that behavior.

I guess my mom took the first train to get back and this how they got back together.

There were other, similar incidents too, spread throughout the years. These ones I've shared, I feel, may have been the most significant ones for you to get a clear picture of the toxic environment I spent the large part of my life in.

It wasn't all bad though. I did have some moments that helped make daily life a little bearable. I used to travel to Aswan in the summer to stay with my grandmother. That was my favorite time. We would go for picnics and meet my aunt and uncles, take in some fresh air, play with animals, etc. My grandmother had almost everything farm-fresh – eggs, chicken, milk, cheese – you name it. I would sit in the balcony in the morning and wait to see which chicken would lay an egg for my breakfast! Sounds amazing, doesn't it? It was. That's why I loved it so much there.

I spent most of my childhood vacations at my grandmother's house. We didn't really spend summer holidays in the North Coast or in any other beach areas like my other friends would. We couldn't afford it back then, especially when we had to get rid of the car and the driver, and later on my dad had to sell the shop as well as the rest of our stuff.

I also moved after a couple of years to a private school, which was way better than the other one and it was where I spent my prep school years.

Arabic culture, which is changing nowadays but surely still exists, used to feel a little strange to my mind. Back then, before anyone showed any interest in what I did, they would first ask me what my dad did – not my mom. The man and his career were most important, and then came the woman. And if the woman was a housewife, that was absolutely fine, sometimes, even better. Only then would they start to judge me – which class of society did I come from? What kind of education and society level did I present? How important could I be to them? And so on. Do you now see why me telling my friends that my dad was a driver was a big, no a *huge* thing? So, I ended up lying about my dad's profession. I cared so much, as my mom taught me, about what would people say.

Here is the thing now, I realize that I was looking then at so many materialistic factors that didn't matter too much. It's quite likely that he did what he did so he could afford my school and keep me at the same level that I had been brought up in. My mom, I only realized much later, cared about how society would look at us to protect me, and herself, from being judged in any way, but can you see how much insecurity *that* would bring to my dad? And how unappreciated would he feel?

Remember, your parents are doing the best they can with what they were taught about life when they were children, and they teach you and protect you with their own level of awareness.

I know I'm not here to blame anyone for what happened, I'm here to learn from my past, and decide who *I* want to become.

3

WHAT MY ADULTHOOD LOOKS LIKE

Prep School was fun – lovely, lively days. Enrique Iglesias was my Prince Charming (come on! Don't judge me, guys). The teachers and school rules were different. I liked my friends – they were streets apart. I had a friend who was the prettiest girl in the school – if she woke up and came to school without washing her face, she would still be the prettiest girl in the school, she looked like a doll! Her dad was our English teacher. His daughter, my friend, was not that interested in studying, as a result, she was repeating the last year of prep. Truth be told, she is the one who introduced me to smoking.

Some kids are more often trying some stuff just to impress their friends or to be cool – just something different, a new adventure, an interesting experience, or whatever you call it. I, however, liked smoking. I started smoking when I was 13. My friend was on another level of trying things. Luckily enough, I drew my limits. I wasn't playing any sports, so I decided to join the aerobics class at school for dancing. We would do some choreography with some aerobic moves and basic belly dance moves. I met a violinist who was playing in the school music classes. He was super skinny and older than me by five years. Back then, for me, he was charming. Of course! That he was an artist and that he was older (and thus wiser and different from the other kids at school) made him even more attractive for me. I hadn't had much of a father figure in my life, so he was almost perfect. All my friends kept telling me that he was older than I, that he wasn't that good looking and that he walked really slowly! Really? What did him walking really slowly have to do with me dating him? I ignored all that and ran to my mom and told her the story. That wasn't the first time I had a crush. My first one when I was in prep school – we looked at each other and once he smiled, that was it, he was a boyfriend already! He would call me at home and since my mom would be next to me, I would get all shy talking about homework with him. Wow! If that isn't super cute, what is?!

Well, it was pretty much the same with the violinist. Except that I almost broke up with him because he was blowing a kiss to me.

We would talk and hang out during my break times but never outside school. On the last day of the year, before exams, it was the final day during which I had to present my dancing show. He decided to hold my hand! I freaked out and looked around to check if anyone saw that!

That's how over paranoid I was.

I recall, one day, after finishing the French class that I was attending with my classmates (two boys and I), we were playing in front of the teacher's house, running around and laughing, as we waited for our parents to pick us up. My dad was the first to arrive. As soon as I got into the car, he started yelling at me, saying, "What are you doing playing with the boys on the street and running? You need to behave. Your breasts have already grown!" I can promise you that I looked like an LCD screen in perfect condition when it comes to that! Remember 13-year-old Jenna, from the movie *13 Going on 30*, on her 13th birthday night? Yeah, just like that. I was so embarrassed and humiliated that the moment I arrived home I ran to my mom, and burst out. She tried her best to take the words out of me, but I couldn't repeat what I heard. At some point I calmed down and told her. She went fuming at him, then came back to me, assuring me that I could continue to play with my friends. As you can get from my story here, my mom had the upper hand.

And again, of course, my dad was only trying to teach me how to act like a lady, preparing me for the world as I was growing up, with his own knowledge and in the best ways he knew possible.

Prep school ended, and the violinist was gone with the wind.

Then came the game that was high school. Here we go down that roller coaster. I changed school again and went to a government high school for girls, which was right next to my prep school. It felt like wonderland in the beginning – I had never seen so many girls and various levels of society in one place before – it was a mix of everything really. I'm thankful now for having experienced this myself, so I can have what I have now from first-hand knowledge when it comes to girls. Through high school, I saw girls smoking at the school, heard about pregnancy and abortions, sexual interaction between girls, drugs, sometimes, nerds, gangsters… almost everything. Luckily enough for me, I met a group of girls – they were my classmates – who I found similar to my social level and personality, and we became friends. I could say I had most of my happiest moments with them, the meaning of pure happiness and innocence. One of them was the closest to me, and still is. She was, and still is, so pretty. Her hair fell to her back so she used to tie it up in a ponytail, and she had this slim supermodel body. Her sense of humor was like no other. We were the bubbly group of the school, most of the groups liked us as we were in our own bubble. Thank God the gangster ones liked us, as we didn't want to achieve anything or compete with anyone; we were just enjoying our lives with pure intention. Our uniform was a white blouse and gray skirt, and the skirt could be long or knee–high. I liked fashion since a young age just like – and thanks to – my mom. One day, I decided that I wanted to make a dress for my uniform, instead of a skirt. Yes, I decided to change the school uniform! I went to the tailor and asked him to make my new dress. It was kind of a baggy thing with a single big pocket in the center of the chest. I started wearing it to school. In a couple of weeks, suddenly, a few versions of the dress came up – some super short, others super tight, some with bling-bling accessories – and the dress was not cute anymore. Then the school wanted to know who invented this idea? Eventually, I got called to the office and was told, in no uncertain terms, to not to wear this dress again. Well, at least I tried. Right?

I had a friend from prep school who was three years older than me. When we graduated, I went to high school and he went to college. His college was near my house, so I used to take my group of friends and hang out with the college boys, with my friend and his new friends. Soon enough, this friend and I started to get attracted to each other. We started talking on the phone late at night, he used to play football with my neighbors in the street under my balcony. I was not allowed to go out often, so only once or twice a month, I would go out with him and his close friend, and sometimes my mom would send my brother with me.

He was the first one for me to hold hands with. Finally. We were together for a year or maybe a bit more. Then we broke up, let's just call it that for now. I will explain more about relationships in my culture later on.

That was pretty much about the 1st year of high school where I could also decide which subjects I wanted to study for the next two years, whether literary or scientific. I chose literary because I liked psychology and I couldn't study it if I chose the scientific section.

The next two years were the most important of all my years of study, as this is where it would determine which college I was going to. This was also the time when my mom was on top of the game as a stalker – she had nothing else going on in her life at that time other than making sure that I was attending my classes. All my friends were very afraid of my mom because if she caught me not attending a class or school, she would call up their parents! No one was allowed to even visit me at home, and this is where my strong stubborn personality started to show even more. The conflict between my mom and me kind of went viral! We would shout at each other and scream, and sometimes we would hit each other as well. One day I came back home later than the time she asked me to get back at. I found her waiting for me behind the door with a pair of scissors and she started pulling my hair and cutting it haphazardly. Another time she cut my clothes because she was mad at me for something. And the story goes on and on. At the same time, my dad was like a stranger to me. I didn't like to talk, sit, or even eat with him. His habits of smoking heavily in the house, burping (he knew I hated burping, and he would *still* do it to piss me off if I was around), eating sloppily and with loud, smacking sounds which were not acceptable to me, or by any food etiquette I know of, and which would suppress my appetite – all of these added to the gap created between me and him.

This is when the house became an absolute nightmare for me.

What I would do when everything was out of my control? I would leave the house, run away and stay with any of my friends. Our family relations with our relatives were not so great on dad's side and they started to fade with time on mom's side as well. What I did not know back then, is that my parents had some of the strongest narcissistic personalities you have ever seen. Sure enough, I picked up some behaviors from my mom at that time – remember, she was my hero.

Some narcissistic personality behaviors, in case you'd like to know, are that they are people who want everything to work their way and no other way. They need to be in total control. They believe they are always right, and some of them play the victim role once a finger gets pointed at them or things don't work their way. They manipulate other people and target their weak points.

They feed themselves on other people's energy, and are even called "energy vampires".

I always knew that my mom's controlling attitude and my dad's ignorance wasn't right, and since I had no authority or power over them, I would just leave the house. They would then look for me by going to my friend's houses, sometimes my mom would even call the police to my friends' homes if they didn't guide her to where I was. That was how she would end up bringing me back home. My mom always cared about "What would people say if you left the house or dressed up inappropriately?" It is a very big deal in my culture if a girl leaves her parent's house. People start judging and say, "Her parents didn't know how to raise her. Where did she go? Did she leave for a boy? No man will now marry her." All of these judgments and assumptions. By 'people', here, I mean neighbors. And so, I always reacted to my mom with things like "I really don't care about them! *They are not feeding me or paying for my school or anything. You, on the other hand, are always shouting and screaming with me, my brother, or with dad. Don't you think the neighbors can hear that? What do you think they think of you? So why don't you ask yourself that question?"

Again, I only got to know later that each of them was only trying to protect me and raise me in their own 'right' way. That was *the* way they thought of at that time with their level of understanding and awareness.

Life went on. At one point, my group of friends and I met three sisters, each one with her own beauty. They were all blonde, with green eyes, but with different features and characters. They were loving, kind, and so welcoming. I mean really welcoming – they would welcome different type of friends, or even people they just met to their house. The middle sister was the closest to me. I will never forget the amount of love she used to shower me with. Their mom had passed away when they were little. They grew up living in a big old house with their dad, brother, uncle, and grandmother. They were taking care of each other and a few stray cats and dogs. No one, however, was taking care of the house and keeping it – or them – clean. It was one of the strangest lives I'd ever seen, and so it had a special attractiveness. In the beginning, my group of friends and I started to go to their house after school for some time before we went back home. Then, we started to skip school to go there. I actually once talked my friends into jumping from over the school fence. We did succeed in doing so, only I sprained my ankle while jumping over. However, that still did not deter me from going to my friends' place and spending the whole school day there. Even though I was in pain, the amount of laughter and joy we had, made bearing all the pain worthwhile. I ended up with a bandaged foot for three weeks. During that time, the middle sister would come for the first few days to change my bandage and aid me with everything necessary until I got better. When we were in their house, we would just go get breakfast and smoke all types of cigarettes available, dance, dress up, gossip, and dream about what we wanted to do in our lives.

I was skinny at that time – tall with long curly hair. We were all kind of different in looks, age, and dreams. We all had the same goal though. Happiness.

One day, the youngest sister of the three decided to introduce us to some hash (a type of drug that is very common in Egypt) she had managed to get. She was always trying to show us that she was the coolest. I guess as she was also carrying more physical weight than all the girls around her, she was just trying to belong and cope with the group of older girls. We rolled the hash in a cigarette (or she did). It was a small joint in relation to the number of girls smoking it. It was not enough for everyone, so most of us, including me, got the chance to have only a puff or two. When I had my share, I complained that it made no difference. Absolutely nothing! Half an hour later, I was supposed to go home. On my way home, soon as I went outside into the fresh air and the wind from the window blew into my face, I started to feel so high. My muscles loosened and I wanted to keep smiling for no reason. This was my first small introduction to the hash affect. And this was also the start of my trip with hash – from time to time we would gather and just share some together.

One day, the sisters and I planned a day trip to the beach over the weekend. That was a special day for me. It was about a one and half hour drive from Cairo. We were a big group, we were so excited and from the moment we arrived, we had so much fun. I met my boyfriend at that time there. We were swimming, listening to music, dancing, when I realized there was a guy who hadn't taken his eyes off me since we had arrived! He was with his friends, they all looked older than me, and they definitely didn't seem to be locals. He had blonde bob hair, was tall, fit, and had one of the most gorgeous smiles I have ever seen. The best, though, were his dreamy, honey-colored eyes. His eyes and eyebrows looked exactly like Tom Cruise – just the eye colour was different. Just before we hit the road back to Cairo, he approached me and started a conversation. He was of Palestinian origin, but born and raised in Canada. This was his first year of university studying medicine in Cairo. "Handsome *and* smart! It is my lucky day then," I had said to myself.

We dated for two years while he was studying in Cairo. We used to meet after my classes on the weekends. He lived an hour and a half's drive from where I did, and that was without traffic. With traffic, it could easily take two hours. Traffic notwithstanding, he used to come to me every weekend once or even twice, to just see me for two hours and go all the way back. Remember? I was not allowed to go out…

All my friends were crazy about him. Boys on the street were jealous of him, he was that handsome. Girls flirted with him even when I was with him.

He is the one with whom I tasted my very first kiss.

He went back to Canada each summer. We stayed in touch by emails every day – sometimes all day. It was the first long distance relationship I had had. That relationship is the one that I haven't been able to forget until date. Funnily enough, we broke up for some reason that I can't even remember.

That was pretty much high school for me. Going out, escaping school and cutting classes, smoking, sometimes clubbing, same friends, same fun as long as I was outside the house.

Then came along college. My high school score wasn't that high, and that didn't give me too many options. My mom didn't want me to go to the same college with my best friend because she thought my friend was the biggest reason for me not achieving a higher score in high school. She wanted me to attend a government academy and study social services. One of the lowest degrees and academies I could get. Even though my score would send me somewhere way better, but private. I don't know if it was money or a way of punishment because of my score, or even both, which led my mom to apply for me at that academy! As I absolutely refused to apply, she had to apply on my behalf. I ended up not going for any registration. I said I'm happy to stay with my high school grade and no power on earth would force me to study there.

With a mix of my stubbornness and my mom's, I ended up not going. My profile was still registered at that academy. My mom thought that if I saw my friends going to college, that would influence me and I would give up and attend my classes at the academy. Of course, that didn't happen. I ended up losing one year without studies. And because she wanted to see me at my best, and she wouldn't be happy that I hadn't attended college, especially after she graduated from a big university herself, she gave up.

I started working at the life insurance company that year and started to become very career-oriented since then.

The next year my mom dusted off my file and sent it to another private academy, specializing in information systems. IT had never been my desire. However, it was better than what she had enrolled me for earlier and was similar to what all my friends were studying. The good thing at that academy was that I didn't have to attend any lectures as I shared before, just the mid-terms and finals. I would study a couple of weeks before the final exams and that would do. And, I could focus on building my career experiences.

That year I met another boyfriend. He used to be my neighbor. He used to flirt with me when I was in prep school, every time he saw me coming back on the school bus. In high school, he was the boyfriend of one of my classmates as well. She was more of a classmate than a friend. She was in our big group of mutual friends. When she announced that he was her boyfriend, I was like… "What! No… you can do much better," I never really liked him from the time we were little kids playing together.

Let's fast forward to my second year in college which was my first at the IT academy. There was a café in front of that academy near my house. That café was owned by the dad of one of our friends. I asked him if I could work as a waitress there, and he accepted straight away. I didn't really care much back then about the quality of the place anyway. I just wanted to learn new experiences and, of course, earn my own money.

All of my friends were really proud of me. My friend whose dad owned the café was a close friend of my potential boyfriend. Both the boys were friends of two of my girlfriends from the big group at school. I didn't know it then, but as he wanted to impress me any way he could at that time, he asked to work as a bartender at the café. The owner's son, too, said he wanted to be a waiter and one of the girls in the group wanted to become the cashier. I ended up influencing the three of them to work and earn their own money. That was their first time working. While it was fun and beautiful to work with friends, the girl was not really my favorite. I always felt uncomfortable around her personally, but she was OK to work with.

Now started the chase. He was crazy in a good way. I will never forget about this boy. He started to tell me how much he had liked me for years, which I knew, but I still said no. He would talk to me again and again, make eye contact, hang half of his body out of his car window in the middle of the street while he was with his friends on my way home and scream "I love you". I remember he would drive the car near me until I got home safe. He would make my coffee in the morning once I got to work. He did all this, he did so much more, but it was still a no for me. He talked to my brother, told him that he loved me. My brother didn't like him at the beginning as he was known as "the bad boy who smoked hash and had many girlfriends," etc., but then he realized that he was serious about me. It was after much doing, that I started to like him. I started seeing that he had actually a funny, charming personality. He was kind, tall, had beautiful eyes, and was very energetic. I accepted to go out with him, then we started dating. All the girls at our new group of his friends were shocked to see him caring and loving and making so much of an effort for a girl in front of everyone. They told me this was because he never used to care. Now, all he wanted was to see me smiling and that was it. He would kiss me in the middle of the street, and we didn't care about the world. He would carry me on his shoulders and walk me through one long downtown street back and forth. Even though his face would be red, and he would be sweating as if he'd just had a real workout, and hardly breathing, he would still be happy doing it. People on the street would be clapping and whistling for him. Even if it was late at night and I was craving something, in less than half an hour he would go get whatever I wanted, in addition to some cookies and savories I liked and would call me to pick it up. He was open-minded, he never said anything about the way I dressed up, even though at the time I wasn't wearing revealing clothes or anything, but the society I lived in would consider miniskirts, jeans and short-sleeve blouses, revealing. I would go out clubbing and dance with my friends, he would never say a thing as he trusted and respected me. This despite the fact that in my society, a girl is really not allowed to go to a bar or a nightclub. There wasn't any argument about who I was out with, where I'd been, and so on. I'd say it was one of the healthiest relationships I had had so far. He used to dream of where we were going to live, how our house would look like, and how our kids would look like. He even came and proposed for me to my mom, as she had to decide whether he could meet with my dad or not. My mom and my brother loved him. His parents liked me, I would say. They told us after the grade results of that year, the engagement would happen. I was very career-oriented back then. It felt like everything was moving too fast. I liked the idea of getting married, but I felt that it was too early. I loved him, but I wasn't ready just then.

Later on that year, my parents got divorced again. It was so messy that the situation got escalated to the police. That, unfortunately, was the only way my dad would leave my mom. It was a very tragic event for all of us.

Thankfully enough my boyfriend was with me at that time. He supported me, and basically calmed the whole situation down for me. Once the divorce was finalized and official and my dad left our life, I couldn't have been happier. But of course, my mom and I were still always fighting, but now it was only one person that I had to deal and battle with.

Soon I started working as a waitress and hostess at one of the fine dining restaurants that was owned by one of the famous actors from back home and a very elegant businesswoman. Remember that restaurant manager who didn't like me because the owner was giving me special treatment, and *he* saw me as a threat to him and his job? Yeah, that's the one. If I were to compare the level between working at that restaurant and the café, they were extremely unlike each other – from customer's category to food and drink quality, to the all-round presentation of the place. I had to leave because of my exams. Meanwhile, my boyfriend and I broke up as I wasn't ready for something as seriously long-term as marriage, and he started to give up on us as well. Which was fair enough. I also heard rumors about the type of relationship between him and his best friend, some people used to say it had become intimate. I also saw the best friend arguing with him a couple of times. And when I asked him the reason, he answered that his best friend felt that I was taking him away from his friends. This was even though the best friend (the waiter) had a girlfriend back then (the cashier girl). Unfortunately, and sadly enough, in my culture, homosexual relationships are completely forbidden. So, whether it was true or not, I absolutely have no judgment on that at all. I still carry love, respect and appreciation for that beautiful man.

I then carried on with my career improvement, from job to job, from one experience to another until I finished college and started having full-time jobs. Every single experience has taught me something that walks me to the next chapter.

I mean, how will you move forward if you're not growing, evolving, and expanding?

Part III

4

THE FLIGHT ATTENDANT PHASE

Many girls and boys in their early years, and I was one of them, dream of traveling the world over. Since graduation, I wanted to achieve that dream – travel all over the world for free, meet new people, different cultures, and wonderful cities and places.

I was 22, working at a petroleum services company. One weekend, after a long day at work, I decided to go to the bar next to the office with my colleagues to have couple of drinks. I met one of my old clients who told me about one of the most famous aviation companies in the world. He asked me why I wouldn't work there, as I met all the criteria for that job? I simply answered, "You know what, you're right. You're not the first one to suggest that to me. I guess I just love what I'm doing at the moment and I'm also well compensated. However, I will apply." Long story short, I applied, and I got the job that would help me fulfill my dream.

And it started with a random conversation at a bar, or, who knows, maybe even a little bit earlier.

A couple of months later, already 23, I joined the aviation industry. I moved to the UAE – the country with the biggest, newest, tallest, and best of everything. The city is absolutely amazing, very luxurious, high-quality public transportation and so on. The UAE easily boasts of high-end hotels, beaches, lounges, clubs, bars, fine dining, and what have you. Even their public beaches are very fancy. It is a full-on luxurious lifestyle, I'm telling you. And yet it also has a very strict and organized system.

That was my first time to leave home and live abroad. Lucky girl, aren't I? It was my first time to have a roommate and start cooking for myself and wash my own clothes, to take care of my own shit basically. My first roommate was Greek, we got along and we became friends. I met people from so many nationalities and cultures at this time. We were about 24,000 flight attendants from more than 140 nationalities, and so I reached a point that I was meeting and working with crew members for the first time on each and every flight I ever operated! In order for us to stay part of that number as qualified and certified flight attendants, we had to go to a training college.

It wasn't easy, I must say. There was so much to be learned within six weeks. And this on my first time away from family and friends. Yes, it was quite challenging in the beginning.

I was the only Arabic girl in my classroom – and totally not the typical, "conservative" Arabic girl that they might have expected. I was all over the place, jumping, dancing, singing, full of life with not a care about what people would say. I was so free, that I'm sure it must have hurt everyone stuck in their own cages and unable to fly. So I had my own challenges because of my transparency.

Even when I was working with Western people back home, there was a slight racism towards the Islamic religion and the Arabic culture, but still they loved Egypt and Egyptians. It is said that our culture has a warmth they have never experienced anywhere else. However, when I moved to the UAE, the antagonism and prejudice towards the Arabic culture was very obvious to me from a lot of people I met. I believe it was that strong because of what they have heard and seen from the media and news or some Arabs. So, they are generalising. For most of them, it is their first experience living in a Middle Eastern country. I wouldn't blame them for their ignorance and generic judgment, as rigidity, restriction, racism, and judgment in the Arabic culture itself *does* exist. I, myself, was ignorant and racist towards certain nationalities as well and would judge people by where they came from.

To become aware enough, educated enough to evaluate a person by their actions and behaviors, rather than where they came from or what they believed in, takes a lot of understanding and acceptance of the self first.

After graduating from the training college, I started to travel. I was so open, yet fragile to the new world that I was about to experience.

What helped me, I think, was that I was blessed enough to have experienced different cultures, lifestyles, and mindsets when I was back home. Those experiences helped me a lot when I moved to the UAE. When someone comes to a different and unfamiliar culture from the one they know of, they feel disoriented and they want to belong, but they struggle if they see and focus on the differences. I guess that is what is called "culture shock". Yes, UAE is an Arabic country, but the locals constitute only around 20% of the population. That makes it a country with one of the world's highest percentage of immigrants or expats. So, we don't meet or interact with only the same culture or nationality. We don't speak our own language that often either!

I must say this had an impact on me too. For me to not lose my connections, to stay connected to who I was, I started having Arabic friends around me. It was to remind me of my friends back home. Naively, I expected the same type of friends that I used to have, only even more free as they had traveled abroad and lived alone like me. Open-minded, free-spirited, without judgment and without breaking boundaries. But the complete opposite of what I expected happened. I didn't feel that I belonged and I started to feel that something was missing. I had friends from the West who I felt more connected to. But still, I started to feel homesick. Changing my whole lifestyle and getting out of my bubble and into new habits, a new lifestyle, new places, and people played a massive role here.

Hence, I decided to spend my time on defining who I wanted to be, what I wanted to do, and who I wanted to spend my time and energy with. I had to detach myself from a lot of people around me as we had different interests in life. I was on an ongoing mental growth-path.

I was learning, traveling, and meeting hundreds of new people almost on a daily basis; however, what I was doing, what I was learning, and the kind of information I was consuming determined my own growth or else I would easily remain in my comfort zone.

My job was one of the easiest jobs someone could ever do, but when it came to sleepless nights, haphazard sleeping patterns, and an upside-down eating schedule because of different time zones, it was quite challenging. Otherwise, I went on the flight, did the meal and drinks service, then went to the desired destination, saw the sights, tried the local food and got back! Heaven, isn't it?

You didn't really work your brain much with that job. Once you got familiar with the nature of the job, it became a built-in habit and we went on "autopilot mode" pretty much all the time. Then it really depended on what we were learning and investing our time in. Some people would learn a new language, some would study something or read a book, others would take that journey as a step to prepare them for the next one, some would just have loads of affairs, multiple partners and non-stop sex, and some would go out partying and life would be good.

I've learnt that whatever you choose will grow inside of you as long as you feed it with your energy and focus. It will become your new built-in habit.

I was young and brimming with life. I started to go to the gym which I had never gone before when I was living in Cairo. I started to learn how to cook. I was going out all the time because I loved to dance. I started to party and go clubbing and drinking all the time – I had so many friends and stamps on my passport from all over the world. Then, the more I grew – older and wiser, the more I became aware of who I was surrounding myself with and what I was investing in and doing with my time.

I started to prefer going to a lounge have a drink and a proper conversation with a friend, than go to a club where we wouldn't be able to hear each other, where the crowd was going to be very disturbing anyway.

Then year after year passed by quickly and the experience was something that I still sometimes can't put in words as I feel it wouldn't do it justice. Really, what kind of job would give you a weekday off on the beach (it's like a weekend on a weekday, isn't it?), let you live in luxurious hotels most of your days, or let you get your lipstick from Paris, your bag from Italy, and even your stockings from the UK? Why stockings, you wonder? Well, because they were cheaper there, and decent quality.

Let me paint a picture for you. I'd be getting ready to fly tomorrow night and go have a pizza at the Piazza Venezia area, in downtown Rome, and on the weekend, I'd have tickets for the Hamilton Broadway show in Chicago.

The lifestyle is really addictive, and we start to struggle to leave that comfort zone. I will speak later about "comfort zones" in detail.

The longer I did that job, the more I opened up my mind, my heart, and my soul. I started looking at so many things from different angles and learned my biggest lessons through people and situations that crossed my way.

Racism was one of the biggest lessons I learned about thanks to that job. Let me explain something that we may not think about every day. Racism is everywhere in the world and, at the same time, racism exists only inside one's mind. People consume it and install it until it becomes fixed in their head – to a point that they are not even aware of it anymore. For example, at any interaction or introduction to someone new, these fixed viewpoint people won't ask about that person's name. The first question they will ask is, "Where are you from?" And then they will start to judge them from this point onwards (that is because they judge themselves in the first place). If the other person behaves in any way that doesn't fit in with the beliefs of the fixed-view person, the first thing they say is, "They did that because they're from so-and-so." And that's just a general example as some people ask this question out of curiosity.

And that leads me to another almost similar lesson I learned. We all come from different cultures, we all have different beliefs and traditions, and whatever you get offended by, could be absolutely normal for someone else. For example, the famous worldwide peace sign with the index and middle finger in a V sign is considered as a middle-finger swear in Ireland and Iran! Get my point? So, basically, whatever you believe in and whatever you get offended by, could be absolutely normal or total nonsense to others. So, be flexible and avoid taking things personally – even if it is something related to the same culture or has the same meaning, it still has nothing to do with you.

This leads us to another lesson I learnt: any human's behavior, action or reaction, is coming from their own model, their own view of the world. Let's say someone does something that we believe is inappropriate or rude. When we get involved and get affected by it in a negative way, it means that we took it personally. Something inside of us has been triggered and that's why we are getting offended and taking action against it. An incident in the sky might help relate to this better. One time, a customer wanted to have beef and we ran out of it. The customer got really angry. Now, we were 40,000ft above the earth, in the middle of the sky. We can't really open the aircraft door to get beef from the nearest butcher even if we wanted to. The customer knew that, yet got so angry – it was almost as if he didn't eat the beef right then, he was going to lose a piece of his heart with it! Of course, as customer service-oriented people, we understand that he paid a certain amount of money to get what he paid for. "This is not the first time this has happened to me, this service you're giving me sucks," he said. Does his frustration come from us as people? Or from the service that he is not satisfied with? Why, then would I take it as a personal attack? Unless something got triggered inside of me, right? That customer was probably having a challenging day already and was just getting more in his way. The cherry on top of that messy cake was that piece of beef.

And that leads us, my beautiful readers, to another lesson. When we start taking things personally, who gets the most affected? Us, right? And if we stretch our thoughts a little more, if we start to take to heart the things we have no control over and have negative thoughts and feelings over them, will that change anything at all? No, it wouldn't. But, if we start looking at it from different angles in order to serve ourselves better and feel good, that could be great way to be able to shift our feelings, right?

I spent seven years in this phase of my life, travelled over 50 countries and more than 120 cities and learned lessons of a lifetime. I lived my life to the fullest, and grew mentally and spiritually in a way that no other career or job would allow me as this one did. I'm forever grateful and thankful that I spent most of my 20s exploring, learning, and evolving, and just before I hit thirty, I made a career shift and followed my heart.

The more I meet people and 'see' them, regardless of their age, color, gender, nationality, or religion, the more I know that we all want to be loved in one way or another. Be at love, so be it.

If you want to know more about my other lessons, keep reading ;)

5

THE ENVIRONMENT

Environment is one of the most significant factors that affects us, including our behaviors and beliefs. The reason why monks go and live in isolation caves and simple austere cells is to avoid the distractions of the exterior world.

Our Culture

Like any other environment, the Middle Eastern culture has its own traditions and habits, its own restrictions as well as beliefs.

Before I go ahead, I do want you, dear reader, to know that all of what I will be sharing further is largely a generality of images and rules about Middle Eastern societies. There are, of course, exceptions to the rules, as the world now is more open and people are well-traveled. Also, beliefs and religious practices vary from one family to another.

Let me start with some behaviors and communication first. We have this weird belief or behavior, whatever you call it, which is lacking speech etiquette. I once read a book called '*The Art of Speech*' by Dr. Ihab Fekry that explains how conflict occurs and how we fall apart just by using the wrong words when communicating with each other. I personally never understood the lack of etiquette. Thanks to the different cultures that I explored at a young age, I developed an attitude of doing what made sense to me. Let me share a few examples here: When we are talking to a family member, a friend, a colleague, or even the security guy, we break boundaries and cease using etiquette with them. We don't say please when we ask for something or thank you when we receive it. I believe that it should be the opposite. Some Arabic families are used to someone – usually a woman – helping them around the house. They are referred to as "Nanny" or "maid." The nanny gets to do pretty much everything – cleaning, washing, cooking, baby setting, etc. The kids grow up thinking that they don't even have to say thank you, it is normal to be served. They start to get this image that anyone who works in customer service is a "Nanny" as they see their parents doing the same. And if there is no nanny, then the mother will do all the house chores – for instance, preparing breakfast for kids. They eat it without saying "thank you", thinking it is their birth-right to get to have breakfast prepared for them. The closer and deeper we get to know each other, the more we start calling each other unpleasant names. We sometimes don't have any physical distance awareness when we talk to each other. I have experienced someone bringing their face too close to mine as I was speaking to them. I didn't understand it then, I don't understand it now – why would they do that? When did I give the impression that I was hard of hearing or had trouble seeing them that they had to get so close? We interrupt each other while talking without even saying, "Sorry for interrupting." We get louder to just prove some point and that we are right. And when it comes to the blaming, oh boy! It will be like, "You said you were going to call me last week and you didn't! I'm really disappointed." You bump into someone who barely knows you, and one of the first things they will ask is, "Why do you never ask how I am? I blame you for that." And you think, "But did you die? Or why don't you ask about me if I don't?" I've never understood why it has to be blame in the first place?

Another thing about social boundaries, or lack of them, is evident when someone expects you to go out of your way, loan them money, skip your busy schedule, stand by their side even when they are wrong, or even sometimes break the rules just because they have some mutual friends, the same nationality, or any connection with you.

There are many such behaviors that I could list and go on about, but I'm sure I've painted a clear enough picture already.

Let me now introduce you to the Middle Eastern woman, for those of you who find them to be a mystery. A Middle Eastern Muslim woman *has* to be conservative. A lot of women have to cover their hair with a veil, and sometimes the face as well. No tight clothes. Not allowed to go out until late – 10-11 p.m. is very late! Not allowed to smoke or drink alcohol. Not allowed to raise her voice or argue, especially with the parents and specifically with the father, only allowed to say "yes" and "I agree" even if it is not the case. Not allowed to go out with a man who is not a family member. In some families, not even allowed to speak to a non-family member. And, of course, not allowed to date or have sex before marriage. Most Middle Eastern women have to marry a man from the same religion.

Us, Middle Eastern women grow up with that idea that we don't leave our parents' house and live alone like Western families. We live with our family until we get married, then we move to our husband's house. We are very family-oriented and, for the majority of us, our main goal is just to get married, have kids to raise and take care of them. Some women, until today, don't even get to choose their husband, as they are not allowed to date in the first place. The parents choose for them, and it is non-negotiable. They are not allowed to disagree. Some women get locked down if they ever think about getting attracted to a man and having a relationship without an engagement or marriage. Sadly, it is pretty much complicated for the woman because of our overprotective and manly society. A woman is made to suppress her feelings and emotions, hence, whatever she wants to do, she has to do everything in the dark, or behind her parents' back. Even talking to a stranger is mostly not allowed, so, imagine kissing someone who is not her husband, or imagine having sex before marriage. That's it. She might as well be dead, and sometimes she literally is. Most times a Middle Eastern woman who dares to flout social rules lives in complete isolation from life and people. She gets humiliated and insulted by not just society, but also family. Some are even brutally beaten by their parents and have physical and mental scars that remain for the rest of their life. It is *that* serious. A Middle Eastern woman will devote her life to the husband and raising the kids, cooking, cleaning, studying, and teaching until all her youth and energy are exhausted in serving others. By and large, a woman from the Middle East *will* completely forget about herself.

It doesn't end there. Let's talk about sexual and physical abuse. Whether it is someone we know or some random guy on the street who felt it is his right to abuse us, we feel very vulnerable if we talk about it to anyone. Trouble is, even if we do, we most probably get blamed. How? Why? Unlike other areas in the Middle East where it is a must for women to wear a headscarf and in some areas even cover their face in a veil. I was lucky I was never forced to hide myself. When a girl gets sexually abused, some people say, "Oh, she wasn't wearing a veil," or, "She was wearing a veil, but she was wearing tight pants and revealing clothes," or, "Oh, it is because she was laughing out loud on the street with her friends,", or "Oh, it is because of the way she was walking, that is why she got abused."

The funniest – and saddest – part about it is that these judgments mostly are from other woman, usually older ones. It is just that most people, no matter what, are going to put the blame on the woman. I could be walking on the street and be almost as terrified as any other female probably would be in Egypt about getting verbally or sexually abused or even robbed. At one time, it had become normal to hear of someone passing by in a car or on a motorbike, and slapping a girl on her bum, regardless of what she was wearing.

All this starts from a young age. Remember, as I have mentioned earlier, my dad's reaction when he saw me playing with my "male" friends in front of my teacher's house, and how angry he was, as I was becoming a lady in his eyes, even though I was still in prep school! If you noticed, it wasn't as if he cared about my safety or told me it wasn't safe to play on the road when cars were driving by fast, for example. However, he specifically mentioned how conservative I had to be. Unfortunately (for him, I guess), I was never that girl would say "Yes, I agree," and that used to get me in so much trouble like I mentioned earlier. I would say I was able to have a voice "somehow" as my parents didn't set a very good example in front of me to follow, especially when my dad was an extremely closed-minded case.

For the longest time in the beginning when I moved to the UAE, I used to get petrified when a motorbike passed me by. This was despite knowing that the city was very open, had so many citizens from all over the world and had a lot of restrictions, laws, and rules that protect women and the system is very organized in general. I only started breathing free out of my house when I got used to their safer environment.

Things are becoming a little different now. Many women are working as well, but some want to just become housewives and they do so if the husband is financially stable.

Why talk about women alone. Let's also look at the Middle Eastern man. The Middle Eastern man is able to stay late outside the house, and travel by himself. The Middle Eastern man also is able to date freely. Even if his family discovers it, it is not considered a big deal. Sometimes the Middle Eastern man is also allowed to date a girl, despite his family not seeing her as 'wife material'.

The man has the upper hand in the house, as he is the household's earning member. He pays for utilities, education, food, etc. In a few and far between cases, the wives have also started contributing these days, especially if the man is unable to afford all the expenses all by himself. A Middle Eastern Muslim man is also allowed to marry up to four women at the same time and any or all of them can be non-Muslims as well. I remember my neighbor was married to two women, one living on the fourth floor and the other on the fifth, and they both seem to still be thriving together. The older I get the more I wonder how they are living in the same building together and how they are friends. It happens, yes, it happens even today, and some women have no problem with it.

That is pretty much the image of the culture and environment that I grew up in.

Did you notice how many restrictions are placed on the woman's feelings, behavior, and voice? Did you also notice the amount of freedom and choices the man could have? However, when it comes to 'voice', neither any woman nor any man has an actual, real voice to express demand their freedom from and express their dissatisfaction over the 'system'. I do understand the restrictions and rules towards the female in my culture come from a place of protection. However, there are extreme and unnecessary restrictions that lead to absolutely undesirable results. I remember when I was in prep, the science teacher had to discuss human genitals one day. Before the class started, she mentioned that if anyone felt shy or embarrassed to attend, they were to dismiss themselves from the class, instead of whispering and giggling. That led to few girls leaving the class because they were too shy or embarrassed! It *is* that bad, yes.

Let me draw a parallel. I have friends from Europe, I asked them if they have a class that explains all that. Of course, they do. They also said they had a photo in their science book that explains penetration. Some of them had separate classes between genders to explain everything – even how to have protected sex. In some countries, their parents had the choice to withdraw them from the class if they were not interested. They also had the option to learn and become aware about it. We don't have a class that talks about love, emotions, and relationships. We don't have a class in school that discusses how intercourse happens and why we feel sexually attracted to each other. It is pretty much the same at home. Children in some families may probably be a little more open with their mother or father when it comes to love and relationships, however, sex still a very sensitive subject and not much of a discussion runs around it. It feels wrong and embarrassing to discuss one of the most important parts in our body that creates life itself! If the discussion does come up among mothers, the mother of an adolescent girl will say, "She is a young girl now. When she gets married, she will know!" And if the girl asks about it, most likely they will start to doubt the girl, and question her about "why she is asking"! The depth and number of suppressed emotions thanks to all these restrictions actually lead to the absolute opposite, as I have seen in so many cases. So, what women usually do, as it is completely forbidden to have sex before marriage, unlike for the man, is to make out and have 'unprotected sex' as we don't have enough knowledge about sex. Before getting married to someone else than their partner, many women would do a hymenorrhaphy, or hymen reconstruction operation, to be able to get married. Another way that the majority of women in the Middle East have found is anal sex, so they remain a 'virgin' till the time of their marriage! Crazy, isn't it? A woman could end up having sex with someone who will probably dump her as he wants to get married to another virgin.

Our social mores and beliefs guide a man to not trust a woman who has slept with before marriage – even if she lost her virginity to him. This whole obsession about virginity has fooled many and continues to do so.

Here is the thing, I definitely do not encourage promiscuous, pre-marital sex. I do encourage education about and around it. Restrictions will never lead to anything positive. I discourage the unfairness in dealing with a woman and a man charged with doing the exact same thing but only one gets the whole blame. Instead of judging her and naming and shaming her, while calling him a playboy, treat them the same by not calling them any names, and by not citing and forcing religious and social tenets on either of them, making them follow it unwillingly.

When love and relationships are discussed properly, and I will do so further and, in more detail, the mind makes sense of why things are required to be in a certain way. And instead of operating from a place of ignorance, fear, guilt, shame, and of trying to fool each other, we will be operating from a place full of self-love and self-respect.

Those were most of the limiting beliefs in the culture that I was born and raised in. I'm sure they do exist in many other cultures around the world too, if not in all of them. The more I travel, meet people and educate myself, the more these flaws become 'visible' to me. Yet I'm talking about my own experience and what I have seen, heard, and learned. I had to mention all of these 'negative behaviors', as some people may call it, so you can understand what I have experienced on my journey to achieve the outcomes that I have reached today.

And for all you women reading this, remember that you are *much* more than you think you are. You are a joyous creature and a symbol of bringing life to light. You need to be treated accordingly. It is your birthright to be treated with love, care, and respect. You have a voice and the right to speak up and live your life freely without any feelings of fear or guilt. You're in this world not only to give birth and raise kids, but also and MAINLY to receive – to receive love and to nourish and glow, to do what you love and dream of doing and not let any society, responsibilities, or rules tie you up, chain you, or drain you. Never let anyone dim your light. You are in control of your life and you're the one who decides how to live it.

You are a whole, complete and perfect just the way you are, and you are more than enough.

The Ego

And then comes in the bigger picture, the Ego. It is our biggest self-distraction. It is the reason for wars and hatred. It affects the way we think, behave, and react instead of realizing that we are a product of our Ego. And by talking about Ego, I mean you, as a human being, you are the Ego, the Ego that always wants to get distracted in one way or another. It is said that 99.99999% of human beings, since humankind was created more than four thousand years ago (some science proves that it is seven thousand years since humankind was created), have died without knowing who they are. And that includes the smartest people in the world, scientists, businessmen, and celebrities. Whether this number is right or not, I would say the majority of people don't know who they are. They get distracted by life. It doesn't matter how smart you are, how successful you are, or how famous you are, we all get distracted – with family, religion, career, money, sex, alcohol, drugs, porn, video games, news and the very many thoughts we have. You name it, everything outside of you is a distraction. Thinking a thought outside of you is a distraction. This book I'm writing now is a distraction, you reading a book is a distraction.

We worry, think, and focus so much on too many matters, mostly external ones, all our lives, until we reach our 60s or 70s and start to wonder, who the hell am I? Why did I do all what I did in my life? By that time, however, we are too rigid, stubborn, and weak to be able to change anything. Then we die without discovering who we really are.

I'm not saying that distractions are bad, there is nothing bad, nothing of what I mentioned is bad, but really, how do you want to live your life? What do you want to do in and with your life? It is all up to you. Let's say right now I'm writing this book, the thing that I'm distracted with now. If I go out with my friends and have some drinks, or go out and consume, inhale, or inject some drugs or even indulge in lustful sex, wouldn't that be a distraction? That's why abstinence is needed, that's why all religions tell us to abstain, and that's why I mentioned monks as an example in the beginning and how they live in caves for years. Abstaining makes you see the beauty of everything, appreciate everything, and feel everything in a way you have never experienced before. I'm not saying leave your jobs and families and go live in a cave or isolation – technically we can't do that, and also our Ego will not allow us to. Our defence mechanism, which is our mind, is too hardwired with all the distractions we have. It is the nature of the mind. Your mind is a more powerful force than a Category 5 hurricane. It is much stronger and more consistent and it will stay with you for the rest of your life.

To know that I had to kick myself out of that hardwired circle, I had to become self-aware in order for me to get to know who I am. I needed to look inside of me, with the help of meditating and breathing. Why meditation? It is a way of mastering the mind, loving unconditionally, letting go of limiting beliefs, staying conscious, and living in the present moment, which I will talk about in more scientific detail later. I'm still discovering who am I each and every day, which helps me to know what serves me and what doesn't, to know what I want and what I don't want, by following my intuition and becoming aware of my own feelings. And, of course, there is an attachment to and distraction by society in one way or another. And it will remain for who knows how long. As long as I live in a certain environment, I'm getting affected by it. How you respond to these distractions and who you let in your life is your own responsibility. At the end, it is you who decide what to become – a victim to what's happening to you, or a master of what is happening for you. Do you want to operate from a place of fear, shame, sadness, guilt, resentment, or anger? Or, do you want to operate from a place of empowerment, love, joy, happiness, compassion, gratitude, and peace?

You see, I had to operate from hate, rage, fear, anger, and resentment and attract all the abuse, harassment, and things I didn't want in my life in order for me to know that it doesn't serve me right. That the more I focus on that, the more I will continue to experience it. I had to operate from a place of love and compassion, make peace with what I have experienced, and attract what I want instead.

And to be able to do that, I didn't have to change the world outside of me, especially when they didn't want to change. Once I changed what's inside of me, the outside world changed.

A lot of people will read this information and will still do what they do and get distracted. But *you* can change yourself and become self-aware. Your quality of living is determined by the quality of your thoughts and feelings.

6

RELATIONSHIP/SITUATIONSHIP

Give the ones you love wings to fly,
Roots to come back and reasons to stay.

—Dalai Lama

Love

What is love? Look it up – it is the most searched question on Google!

What does that tell us? Simply, that people are confused with the meaning and are searching for one. We get attracted to someone, then we like that person and start dating, enter into a relationship and fall in love. After a period of time, things fall apart and we 'fall out of love', break up, and have our 'heartbroken' phase. Then go find someone else, get attracted, like, fall in love, then fall out of love again. And so it goes on.

Everyone is looking for happiness and love. Everyone wants to be happy, loved, wanted, and desired. That is our main drive and we do the things we do just to reach that state, even if we're not aware of it.

So, what is it that is stopping us from reaching where we want, then? Is it the people we choose? Is it their fault? We start chasing answers to questions like, "Were they just not good enough for us?" "Were we way out of their league and are they are going to regret losing us?" Or we start wondering if it is the other way around. "Am I not good enough?" "Am I unworthy of love?" We start believing they are going to find someone else and they are going to love them. That they never loved us, we are unworthy of love, that we're going to remain single forever.

We create mindsets and labels like all men cheat, all women are bitches, and more things like that just so we can boost our Ego and protect ourselves.

There is a story of a blind woman who hated herself just because she was blind. She hated everyone, except her loving boyfriend.

He was always there for her. She would say that if she could only see the world, she would marry her boyfriend. One day, someone donated a pair of eyes to her and now she could see everything, including her boyfriend. Her boyfriend asked her, "Now that you can see the world, will you marry me?" The girl was shocked when she saw that her boyfriend was blind too, and refused to marry him.

Her boyfriend walked away in tears, and later on wrote a letter to her saying –

"Just take care of my eyes, my dear."

Most probably that story is fictional, and hopefully the boyfriend took his eyes back, or at least gave her two slaps or more, I don't know.

What I do know is that we love people because of how they make us feel, what they do for us, and how they fulfill our needs. We seek external attention and validation, we look for it outside of us, and we call it love. And once others stop giving us those same exact feelings, attention, and care that they did in the beginning, we start to drift apart and 'fall out of love'. Was it really love, though? Have you ever been truly in love? If you have, you will know that there is no way out of it. In order for you to understand what 'in love' means, you have to know the difference between conditional and unconditional love.

In a technologized world, pretty much everything is done through technology, even dating. In 2017, for example, I started using Tinder, the dating app.

The second date was my first actual boyfriend! I went to meet him to get to know him as a new friend as he was so funny, even if his photos weren't that great. Yes, funny as it may sound, I used to make friends from Tinder when I was using it. Once I saw him, however, I said, "Oh boy! You are definitely *not* a friend." He was very tall and handsome, one year older than me. I would say he was the second most handsome boyfriend I had after the high school one. He was my first full relationship. Yes, I was waiting for the 'right one'. A bit romantic, I would say. We were 'blindly in love'. At that time, I didn't have anything to compare the feelings with. We were dancing and laughing from the bottom of our hearts. He was the funniest and smartest man I had ever seen back then. I remember that laughing with him was similar to the laughs I shared with my friends in the high school: pure, innocent, and from the bottom of our hearts. All my friends loved him and were complimenting me on how handsome he was. I never experienced what I felt for him with anyone before. At the same time, we were fighting and arguing almost all the time. We used to break up at least once a month. We weren't living together, yet, but each time we fought, I would take my stuff and leave. Remember, that is how I used to confront my problems with my parents – just leave! We both cried together, laughed together, and experienced an intense level of emotions, I would say. He put in a lot of effort and went out of his comfort zone to cope with my full, hyper, energetic lifestyle. But that was not who he truly was. He was also a very jealous man. And I was a very controlling woman who wanted everything her way or he could take the highway. So, we broke up and 'fell out of love', and that was the first and most painful heartbreak I have ever had so far. I felt that I would never be able to love or feel that feeling again. I felt that the world and time had stopped. I deeply suffered and for the first time, and fortunately the last time so far, I experienced a panic attack. Moving on from that relationship was the hardest thing I ever had to do. Months passed and I was trying hard to pick myself up again.

Then, one day when I was at the airport in India, I saw a glimmer of light and the first step to my new journey. A book called *You Can Heal Your Life* by Louise Hay. I looked at it, it looked at me, we got attracted to each other, then it was love at first sight all over again. I should let you know that we are still in love from that very moment, and I believe that we – the book and I – have that harmony between each other, like with no one else. That was my first ever AHA! moment of my new journey. To make it more harmonious, another girl who was travelling with me liked what she saw and wanted to get the same book. She was missing some money, I think $4.50, I can't remember accurately, and I had that exact $4.50 in my pocket left! I gave it to her so she could get the book.

Prior to this, I had no clue about childhood and adulthood conditioning, how I could actually heal myself, and even how to breathe! Yes, I had watched the documentary *The Secret* when I was a teenager, but that was different. Bit-by-bit, as I read the book and applied it to my life, I started to love life and open up again. Then I got distracted by it. I didn't give myself enough time to heal, and voilà! Within only ten months from my previous situationship, I fell in love again. It was another Tinder date. This time, however, it was different. I was more aware about the law of attraction and what healing and intuition mean, and how it works.

Intuition is when you know something *before* you think. It is that inner feeling that tells you something is comfortable or uncomfortable, without any facts or data supporting your feeling. You can pick up on things or people's vibrations or vibes state which will cause you to feel whether someone or something is positive or negative based on your model of the world. In simpler words, it is the gut feeling you have towards an event or a person – whether it is a good feeling or an uncomfortable one. From the moment I met that man, my gut feeling told me NO, DON'T! However, I closed my eyes and completely ignored that feeling, like so many of us do. I fell in love with his eyes – they had a trapped child inside, a child full of pain who did not know how to grow out of it. I said to myself, I have tried bad boys before, let me try a good one. Once again, I felt that *this* is real love, and this is how it should be. I loved him not only with my heart, but with my mind and soul. I made so many efforts and broke so many boundaries that I hadn't with anyone before, and so did he. He was five years older, very cute, had a small body, but a huge sense of humor! He was a kind, loving, polite and well-mannered, beautiful man. This was my first time living in with someone and experiencing a real, complete relationship. I proposed and he said, "Yes! You are the first one I have ever thought of getting married to." But he didn't trust that I would stay with him, especially, that I would pack my stuff and leave with every fight. I started to become very insecure, and that wasn't my usual behavior. I started to become someone else I didn't even know, and so did he. Manners, kindness, and cuteness were thrown out the window, and we 'fell out of love'. He wasn't ready to be in a committed relationship either, as later on I found out that he was cheating on me. I think I had known from the beginning that there was something not right and I ignored the 'red flags'. By then I was not a situationship innocent anymore, as the first one had been my biggest lesson and greatest teacher. And that is why when this breakup happened, I had some sense of relief, despite the pain and sadness.

Heartbreak

We tend to use this word without even knowing what it is. Did I really get my heart broken? My heart was never broken, nobody could ever really do that, but they broke my *expectations* – the expectation of having that specific person with me for the rest of my life. It is like desiring an ownership which we never have. I forgot that everything is temporary. I acted as if it was forever and I forgot to live the moment that I was in. I got very spoiled by the relationship I had and built that 'forever' expectation. And in these expectations this person had to be exactly the same way I wanted them to be, they couldn't change, they had to be the same, feel the same and do the same, and fulfill the same needs. They couldn't just go and like or love someone else, they couldn't feel anything else for anyone else, they had to be mine! And that is why I was in pain. Because of my own expectations. This can be applied to breakups, to workplace conflicts and disappointments, to friendships, and even to when someone dies. When someone very dear to us dies, we feel deep heartache for losing them, as they broke our expectations of them living longer. That happened when my grandmother died, and broke my mom's expectations.

What we tend to do when our expectations are unfulfilled is to get distracted, get into rebounds, go out every night, get drunk, and mess around. We talk about it in a way to deny our feelings – we say we are 'flower power' and do our best to suppress that pain. While what we really need to do instead, is to feel it, accept it and know that it was real in order for us to truly heal. When we heal, these emotions will heal as well, then we will feel different feelings towards the world and those who once broke our expectations.

The Seven Essene Mirrors

Another question to ponder on here is, "Why did I attract a jealous insecure man or an addict into my life?"

Are they bad people or am I the bad one? Are men in general just assholes? Or do I not deserve to be loved unconditionally? Regardless of our gender, all these questions cross our minds in one way or another when things go to a different direction than the way we desired. You see, I had to attract every single person in my life, whether it was a family member, friend or a romantic relationship in order for me to learn and grow the way I needed to, with or without me knowing that I'm doing it. How will I know a toxic relation from a healthy one unless I try and know the difference? Those people were meant to cross my path and we were meant to spend some time together, so I could know what they were triggering in me and where I was still stuck in my life. They also helped me see what I want in my life and what I don't want.

I have been told that I attract a reflection of me into my life at any given moment. That didn't sit right in my head, as some relations in my life felt like they had nothing to do with me. Then I peeled the first onion-layer of a whole new world of knowledge and science about the law of attraction and quantum energy fields that I'm still discovering, wandering, and digging deeper into. Let me share with you an introduction to the reasons behind the relationships that happen in our lives. Gregg Braden has explained it by saying that The Ancient Essenes[1] have perhaps identified best, the role of our personal relationships. They categorized them into seven mysteries of relationships, each of which we will experience life through one or another of these relationships. They categorized these mysteries as mirrors. What the Ancient Essenes remind us of is, that each moment of our life, the reality that we have become within is a mirror to us, is a reflected reality. It is mirrored to us by the actions, choices, and the language of those around us.

Mystery of the First Mirror: The Mirror of the Moment

This is the mirror of what or who we are at the present moment. What we send to those who are closest to us in that moment? Do we feel anger or fear? We will then mirror anger and fear. Do we feel joy and happiness? We will then mirror joy and happiness. The mirror works in every way. What we see in the first mirror is *a reflection of what and who we are in the present moment.*

---

[1] Two to three hundred years before the Christian era, in Alexandria, Egypt there were mystics called the Therapeutae, the healers. They were known for their flowing white robes. They established an embassy outside the walls of Alexandria on the shores of lake Mareotis near Alexandria. In Palestine, they were called the Essenes or Nazarenes, meaning watchers, because they were watching for a high celestial being, they believed was soon to visit earth. Although they were primarily, but not exclusively Jewish, the Essenes were master weavers of Egyptian, Iranian, Greek, and Tibetan ascension practices.

**Mystery of the Second Mirror:
The Mirror of That Which Is Judged**

This mirror tells us about our judgment at the present moment. It refers to the models imposed on us 'subtly'. Which could be some unpleasant experience or unhealed wounds from the past that we didn't forgive or heal. If we judge with emotional charge, then we will attract exactly what we are judging. Let's say if you were surrounded by people in whom a behavior model causes frustration or triggers feelings of anger or bitterness and you realize that these models are not yours at that moment (like my dad's eating habits that I mentioned earlier, for example). If you can honestly say no, there is a good chance that it is showing you what are you judging at the moment.

**Mystery of the Third Mirror:
The Mirror of That Which Is Lost, Given Away,
Abandoned or Taken Away**

This mirror refers to that beautiful sensation we feel when we look into someone's eyes, and we are drawn to them as there is something magical happens, and we want to spend as much time as possible with that person. These magical moments mirror something we have lost, abandoned, or was taken away from us. It is one of the easiest mirrors to recognize because we perceive it every time we are in the presence of this special person. All they need to do is look at us, look into our eyes, and something magical happens at that moment. We feel an electrical charge or goosebumps.

What really happens at that moment? We give up on huge portions of us to survive the experience of life. We lose ourselves, without even noticing, thanks to the control performed by those who have 'power' over us. Through the lens of the third mirror, we are re-allowed access to that lost innocence. When we are faced with those who embody the same thing we have lost in the past and we are looking to reach our totality, our body produces a psychological response, that we call magical attraction, to that person. If you experience that again, which you will, ask yourself, "What does this person have that I have lost or abandoned or that has been taken away from me?" The answer may surprise you since you have, almost all the time, felt a sense of familiarity with everyone who passes your life. It might even surprise you when you get attracted to the same gender, or someone other than your spouse, with whom you feel like you found 'the one', even though you love your spouse to the moon and back.

Mystery of the Fourth Mirror: Mirror of Most Forgotten Love

This mirror is a reflection to our most forgotten love. It could be abandoned or unfinished relationships, or even an experience from past life when an unfulfilled conclusion was established. And hence, life will present to us challenges, relationships, career, friendship, people, etc., that will recreate themselves over and over again – until we get it, get it, get it. This mirror is of a different quality from the other mirrors, as we talk here about compulsive behaviors and addictions. When we talk about addiction, dependence and compulsive, many of us think of drugs and alcohol, which certainly could be part of it, but we are not just talking about them, There are some more subtle and less obvious addictions such as family control, co-dependency, and sex. Often over the years we adopt behavioral models that become so important that we can reorganize the rest of our lives to be able to live with them. Such behaviors are compulsive and could create addiction. This mirror allows us to see and observe ourselves in a state of dependence and compulsion. Through these feelings as we slowly give up and yield to compulsive and addiction, and we end up giving away the things or people that are so dear to us and we love most.

Mystery of the Fifth Mirror: Mirror of Father/Mother
Probably the most intense of all mirrors, it refers to the way we live our lives. This mirror shows us how much our parents influenced our lives. Heavenly Father and Mother, the Masculine and the Feminine, all represent our parents or caregivers. Everything that has to do with how we live our Divinity on earth is related to our parents. Through their relationship with each other or from what we have learned with or from them, our beliefs and vision of God are created. If we feel we are always being judged, or not good enough, it will reflect our relationship with our parents and that we felt judged by them and not good enough. This allows us to see better, and more deeply, why we do the things we do and why we live our lives in a certain way. It shows us our parents and the interaction with them, to prove that our actions reflect our

beliefs and expectations with regard to what is sacred to us, to be specific, our heavenly Father and Mother, the sacred Masculine and Feminine aspects of our Creator. It is through the relationship between us and our parents that we see and realize our beliefs and expectations about God, the Universe, energy, nature or whatever you believe in or that is most important to you.

Mystery of the Sixth Mirror: Mirror of Your Quest Into Darkness

It is called the 'dark night of the soul'. It is also the place we learn our deepest lessons and find our greatest strengths. It reflects challenges and difficulties that we can overcome with gratitude and ease. In this mirror, we can lose everything – all the walls we have put up around us – be naked and stripped of all external protection before the 'dark night of the soul' so we can find trust in life. It means that every challenge we face in our lives is a test. These are lessons we must learn to reach a 'higher self', no matter how difficult the situation is. We have to always act wisely and calmly, not to react, but respond to things when they happen instead, so that we finally learn whatever we need to from the experience we are going through. As Albert Einstein said, "It is at the time of greatest crisis that we grow and learn more."

Mystery of the Seventh Mirror: Mirror of Self-Perception

It is the subtlest and the most difficult to be accepted. Why? Because it asks us to believe that we are perfect just the way we are. No matter what the outcome be, it invites us to not follow the limits and qualifications or measures applied by others. The only goal and reference in our lives must be ourselves and no comparison with or to anyone else. It is the simplest, yet perhaps the hardest to demonstrate. This mirror shows us that everything that happens in our life is in Divine order. Just know this and manage your feelings about any events and know that the Universe is taking care of everything entirely.

And Now, let's get back to Situationships!

Earlier when I mentioned "power over us", I meant this role, this exact role that we embody from young age. Every single event of our life happened for us, not to us. We are responsible for having or experiencing them. We are more powerful than we think. We create our own reality and attract who we attract to serve our growth and journey in life. We will go into more detail later.

Most people think it is normal to have an abusive situationship and call it a relationship, as this is what they see around them most of the time.

So, they have these limiting beliefs telling themselves that this is the best they can do and thus they decide to lower their standards and stay in that situationship.

Before these two relationships of mine, I dated quite a few men from different cultures, and by mixing all these experiences together I came through with a few beautiful outcomes:

- I need to heal myself before going into anyone's life with a baggage full of past conditioning, as that creates a version of me which was controlling, insecure, needy, and lacking self-love and self-respect.
- We tend to skip one of, if not the most vital elements of all relationships – friendship! We skip the period of getting to know each other as new friends, hanging out, talking, spending some time and doing some fun activities together, learning more about each other's' personalities and characters, seeing if we have the same core values, interest of future, goals, and purpose, building that strong solid platform of rapport, etc.
- Most people judge each other on their physical attributes, how they dress up, how many followers they have, how much money they have, where they live, what kind of car they drive, what they do for a living, "How they will complete them and support them financially and emotionally," and so on! Their complete focus is on outside/external matters and false values, and that is why the divorce rate is very high, as we miss out all those first steps for a relationship where we can learn if we are compatible in the first place or not. Of course, these external things are important and lead a certain lifestyle, but what about this person's character and conscience?

What do they value in life? How do they live their life? Do they look at peoples' lives on Instagram, see how models pose, and spend all their time attached to their phone like it is a part of their extremities, or they are looking for real value in life, investing, and appreciating their time? Many people don't heal, don't even know what they want, and suppress their feelings as they have never been told to express them, especially men. From the time they are little, they get the idea that "men don't cry", that big boys are strong, and that they should tolerate pain instead.

- Abuse becomes so normal. Abuse, in any form is not normal, whether it is physical, verbal, emotional, mental, or sexual. Just because a lot of people do it, doesn't make it right. Cigarettes are not good for your health, right? Most of us agree with that on some level. Yet there are over one billion smokers around the world. We got used to see people smoking so we don't freak out if we see someone smoking, but that still doesn't make it right. It is the same for abuse.

I know people who were in a very toxic marriage for 17 years. My parents were a great example that someone could stay in marriage for 20 years and it could be one of the most toxic environments that anyone could live in. I could give you so many more examples of these, but I also see healthy relationships where you can choose what you can tolerate and what is a deal-breaker for you.

The bottom line here is, you attract the mirror that needs to be healed. If you see yourself in the same rut of familiar behavior from different relationships in your life, it is because it needs attention from you. It needs to heal and be let go of. The Universe will bring the same events and scenarios from different people, playing different roles in your life, until you get it, get it, get it.

Does that make us bad people? No. It makes us humans. This is how humans learn – we make mistakes and learn from them or keep making the same mistakes until we learn the lesson. None of my relationships were ever a mistake. They would be now if I continued to stay in one of them. They were the perfect fit at the right time for me to learn the lessons that I had to learn. I now know that the source of my pain was my ego and its expectations, not the other person.

Situationship vs. Relationship

What I had in my past was a situationship. What I mean by the word situationship is a problematic, unresolved relationship that both parties know that it isn't working out but they still decide to stay in this situation. We didn't really know what unconditional love is. We loved each other yes, but my ex loved his Porsche and house as well. I loved my house and outfits as well.

A healthy relationship is two different people, who are perfect, whole, and complete by themselves, not waiting for anyone else to complete them. They don't think of themselves as half and they don't wait on the other half to complete them. They don't fight. Instead, they disagree, discuss, and negotiate. They do not try to change anyone's behavior or attitude. There is no place for manipulation, deception, cheating, infidelity, etc. There is trust, freedom and respect for each other. I have friends for more than ten years, and we don't fight. Yes, there are misunderstandings and disagreements, but not disrespect. And this is how, I believe, it should be with every relation in my life. Whether it is with a family member, in a friendship, a colleague, or in a romantic relationship.

Remember, Mr. or Ms. Perfect don't exist. No one is perfect. As some wise person once said, our perfection lies in our imperfection. We become a 'perfect fit' for each other by the unconditional love we hold for *ourselves* and by the respect and acceptance for each other. 'Perfect fit' is without judgment and pointing fingers, sacrificing things and habits that make us meet halfway. 'Perfect fit' is trusting and giving the freedom for each other, becoming attentive, caring, and investing in that relationship because we see the value of building it.

Rejection

One of the hardest feedback to the ego and the brain is being rejected. Research shows that the feeling of being rejected is equivalent to a physical pain in the brain. The areas of the brain that are triggered by rejection are the same as those which get triggered when experiencing physical pain. That is why medication for physical pain works the same way for rejection. So, rejection is painful, yes. Why? Because we translate it as "I am not worthy", "I am not enough", "I don't deserve to be loved". That's also why we sometimes get back to the same person who rejected us, as their being with us makes us feel validated and worthy again. They chose us again, we are good and worthy again, etc.

But just because this partner, friend, job, etc., 'rejected' you, does it mean that you are not worthy of love or that you are not enough? If you just answered "yes", to that, please ask yourself these questions: really? Am I sure? Is it the absolute, indisputable, undeniable truth? Are they the major validation that indicates my self-worth? Does them leaving me mean that I'm not good enough? Are they facts and universal truth or just assumptions in my head caused by my own lack of self-belief and their destructive behavior?

Right from the time we are children, we get used to external validation and that's why we are in constant need for it. Once it is been taken away from us, we start on the slide to self-doubt, blame, and losing self-confidence. The moment we truly love ourselves, and have this unconditional love from and within ourself, we will no longer have the need or urge for external validation. We will, ourselves, be the true inner voice of validation, and at one point, we will be thanking this person for leaving room to a new life and experience. I will be talking more about rejection therapy later but know this for now!

I promise you this: you are worthy of love. You are whole and complete with or without anyone else. You are more than enough. You are perfect just the way you are. Them leaving is a blissful lesson and you will fall in love again and again throughout your life. All you have to do is to believe and have faith in yourself.

Unconditional Love

A man was polishing his new car. His four-year-old son picked up a stone and started to scratch on the side of the car. In anger, the furious man took his child's hand and hit it many times, not realizing that he was using a wrench. The child lost all his fingers due to multiple fractures. When the child saw his father, with painful eyes he asked, "Dad, when will my fingers grow back?" The man was deeply hurt and speechless out of his guilt and the child's innocence. He went back to the car and kicked it many times. Devastated by his own actions, sitting by the car he looked at the scratches. His son had written, "LOVE YOU DAD."

Regardless of how explicit and old that story is, sadly enough this is the reality and the majority of our world today. Not so long ago, before all our distractions became so technologized, things were made for people to use, and people were made to be loved. Unlike now, when things are being loved, and people are being used. As a species, we appreciate the materialistic world more than the field of energy which we call humans, who created them in the first place.

We don't hear this word 'unconditional love' that often now, and if we do, do we know what it means?

Unconditional love means that in order for us to love someone else, something else, anything outside of us, we need to, and must, love ourselves first.

How? Simply by being happy with who we are and what we have in that very moment. Loving the self is not only by dressing up and getting ourselves a nice car, a new pair of shoes, or a fancy bag. It is getting to the core of our inner selves and accepting ourselves the way we are. It is not waiting for any external matter outside of us to make us feel happy or loved – a new job, a partner, more money, new things, a new body shape, a new house, or getting healthier. If we wait for, or lean our happiness and self-validation on any of these things to happen, we will be denying our existence right now and right here. Self-criticizing, being in the role of the victim, pointing fingers at our parents and others saying, "it is your fault" will not make us any better. It takes our power away. Take over your role of being empowered and being a joyous, creative expression of life. Know that you will change, but the change you make when you love yourself unconditionally is always positive. Always. Fall in love with yourself and enjoy yourself by being alone before enjoying yourself in somebody else's company. Release all the resentment, anger, jealousy, sadness, and blame towards anyone. Forgive and fill your heart with love, compassion, care, and gratitude. This is when you will truly be in love with yourself and accept yourself exactly the way you are, with the couple of love handles of yours, the little belly, and even any disease you may have. Once you do that, you will be able to unconditionally love everyone and everything around you, and you will have the intimate relationship you always dreamed of. You will love people as they are, not wanting them to change anything, not judging them, just accepting them and not having the urge to control them or have insecurities kicking in. You will have the job you want, the abundance and health you always craved for, and everything will fall into place in your relationships. Because once you taste that feeling, it becomes addictive and you will work every single day of your life to stay in that state of harmony and unconditional love.

And last but not least, by saying, "love and forgive whoever has done you wrong in your perspective," I don't mean you have to keep them in your life. This process is for you and not for them, and this forgiveness is meant to be for your own sake, for your own healing. You want your heart to be filled with love and gratitude without any resentment or resolution of not letting the past go. We want to heal our past to focus on our present, in order to have an even better future that doesn't bring any undesirable patterns. It is absolutely fine to be alone for some time, there is nothing wrong with it. Yes, having a relation will nourish and grow you and support you when it is right. Don't wait for anyone or any half to complete you. Instead, complete yourself and nourish it with the amount of love you give for yourself. Remember if you loved the "wrong" one that much, imagine how much you are going to love the right one – which is you. Forgive them and let them go. If you are in a relationship now, and you feel in any way that it is not supporting nor nourishing you, start to work together on healing. There is always exception to the rule, and there is always a chance for people to change ONLY if they want to.

You are free to do what you feel is good for you and for your life. I'm not here to judge you or tell you what you should or shouldn't do. I'm here to share my own experience and knowledge and you can see and take whatever sits right in your beautiful mind and just simply ignore the rest.

- Remember that you are more than enough. You don't have to do anything that makes you uncomfortable or unhappy just to make someone else happy or because of the fear of losing them.
- Watch the red flags and don't ignore or deny your intuition.
- I once heard a definition of how to evaluate the person in front of you which made so much sense to me. It says: *I don't talk, I don't hear, I don't see, I FEEL.*

Part IV

7

ARE YOU "SMART ENOUGH"?

> "We must be willing to get rid of the life
> we've planned, so as to have the life
> that is waiting for us."
>
> —Joseph Campbell.

Before I go deeper and start discussing the scientific facts behind most of the things that we do, I want to share with you how this drifting journey started. When I was with my ex, we had a very good and ideal lifestyle, dressing up, shopping, date nights, working out, traveling the world, watching TV and going to movies, brunches, cooking, beaches, etc. While to someone looking in from the outside, everything was perfect as there was nothing wrong with it, I still felt that there was something missing. I felt that I wanted to do more and it was the time for me to move on to my next chapter and build my own career. I would come up with an idea almost every week with what I wanted to do, which would lead me to my path of becoming an actress in Hollywood. I started thinking about modelling, dancing, acting classes, etc. but I would forget the idea a week later. Meanwhile, my boyfriend and I grew apart as well. Then, after the breakup, I started to search again for what I truly wanted. I started to watch and read about relationships. One thing led to another and I found an online course for Life Coaching. The course insulted my intelligence, to be honest, as the questions were too easy, and I realized that I'm doing all these things without me paying this amount of money just for online certificate that didn't add anything new to me. I managed to console myself by accepting that it is a step forward, and that I shouldn't underestimate it. I kept at it and on my way, I found a great gem called NLP[2] and Timeline Paradigm techniques. Here started my discovery, knowledge and my on-going, mind-blowing journey.

So now, let me share with you some of this knowledge so you, too, can understand how we function.

---

2 NLP: Neuro Linguistic Programming. To Explain it in simple words, NLP is a methodological set of tools and techniques used to free the body and mind from the chains of negative emotions attached to the past, which helps you achieve what you desire and guides you to where you want to be.

We come into this world with innate abilities and functions that are naturally built in. You didn't have to learn how to grow, dream, digest, heal yourself, or even pick your nose among other things. Apart from these built-in, natural abilities, pretty much everything else has been learned. Talking, languages, walking, what we believe in, what we stand for, what things and people mean to us, etc., are all accepted and adopted from the environment we are surrounded with. In order to learn all that and even more, our nature ability of learning follows the four quadrants of the learning process. The following model is the "conscious competence" learning model proposed initially by management trainer Martin M. Broadwell in 1969.

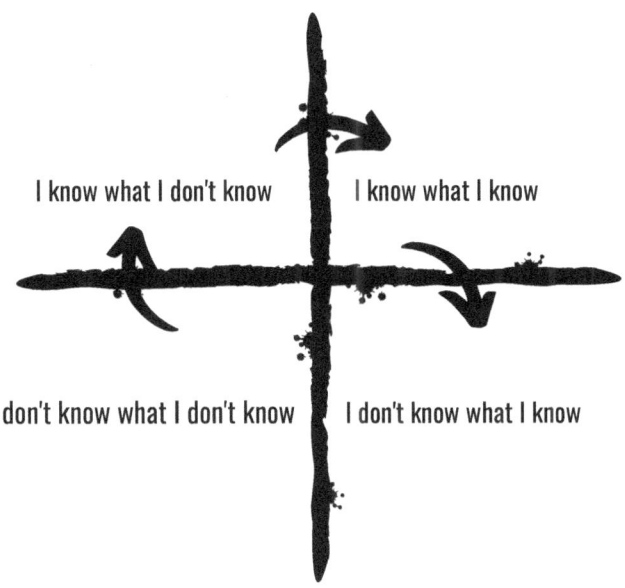

Quadrant 1: I don't know what I don't know.

Have you ever thought of something you are completely ignorant of? 'Blissful ignorance', they call it. It is some thing or a subject or a skill that you were unconsciously unaware of, you had zero clue about at one time, such as the first time you learn a new language or start to drive a car or ride a bike. Then you discovered more about that thing and it 'entered' your life.

That will lead us to the next quadrant.

Quadrant 2: I know what I don't know.

This is the discovery part. It is when you know very little about a certain subject, but you know whether you are interested or not in learning more about that. If not, your learning process about this subject will stop for now. This could happen, for example, if you didn't have enough passion to learn that new language.

But if you are, then you will start digging deeper and ask more questions to get to know more about it and that will lead you to the third quadrant.

Quadrant 3: I know what I know.

Now you are consciously aware about that subject. You know what you know about it. Like when I started to speak English, for example, and knew how to make a whole conversation, or when I mastered riding my motorbike.

Your conscious awareness of how much you know, understand and have mastered that knowledge will transfer you to the fourth and last quadrant of learning.

Quadrant 4: I don't know what I know.

Once you master the subject by repeating it and practicing it again and again, it will become something you are no longer consciously aware of. You will be in the state of what is known as Unconsciously Competence. You will do it with zero conscious effort, as it is now a habit and your body doesn't have to memorize the steps consciously again.

When experts in a field are asked how they do it, they say it is super easy, even though they don't consciously memorize the steps required to do it. Like the famous car example. For those who drive, have you ever experienced that feeling when you drove somewhere and once you arrived, you realized, "I have no idea how I arrived here," as your body was in a 'driving trance'. You might be thinking and doing other things while driving in autopilot mode. Which is exactly the way your brain and body were taught to do things.

This guides you to figure out which quadrant you are in towards any subject. I personally choose to stay in the *I don't know what I don't know* quadrant. Why? I know how to ride a bike, but I don't know the mechanics of it or how to fix it. Any other quadrant will just limit my growth and learning by thinking that I know/don't know that much about that subject. "I don't know what I don't know" gives me more opportunities for my neurology to experience growth, develop and unfold to new realities and learnings, being flexible and open-minded to new possibilities and knowledge.

We are here in this world to either evolve, develop, and unfold, or simply die. Nothing in nature stays as it is, everything goes to one of these directions, and we are part of this universal nature.

Are you 'smart enough'?

And what I mean by that is to ask if you are teachable, if you're smart enough to know that there are other realities outside of you. Because if you are not teachable or open to new realities then you are not coachable. That means no one can really help you at this point.

So, are you smart enough? Do you know how much of that you don't know?

It is very simple to be smart enough, by the way. It is basically approaching every subject with knowing that it is literally not possible to know everything there is to know. In the absence of knowing absolutely everything there is, we should never approach life with the attitude of "I already know it all."

In order for anything, or anyone, else to serve you and help you reach your purpose and get what you want from life, you must approach it with an attitude of "*I know that I don't know what I don't know.*" You will be surprised with how many opportunities and insights can open for you if you look at life from that angle.

Flexibility Measurement

I would like to share with you an exercise that you can do it on your own, so you can self-qualify and measure your level of teachability and flexibility. Bear in mind that your teachability is active and can change from time to time. The higher your score is, the greater is the chance you will be able to learn and change, unlike when it is low, it doesn't give you the same learning feedback and result.

You are going to calculate your flexibility measurement, and you have to be totally honest with yourself to reach the desired result.

On a scale of 0-10, rate your desire and willingness to learn and change in the questions below. Use the sub-questions below each question to guide your chosen rating. Your true results will be when you look inside of you so you may find the honest answer.

1. What is it your willingness to learn? (0-10)
   - What action/s are you willing to do?
   - How much time are you honestly willing to invest?
   - How much of an effort are you willing to put in?
   - How much money are you willing to spend?
   - What are you willing to let go of or sacrifice?
   - What are you willing to give up or quit?
2. What is it your willingness to change? (0-10)
   - How ready are you to change?
   - How flexible and accepting are you of change?
   - How much are you willing to change the way you think?
   - How much are you willing to change the way you feel?

To calculate the result of your flexibility index in a very simple way, multiply the two number outcomes of the learning and change. This will bring you to the total. Minimum will be zero and maximum will be a hundred.

Example:

If your willingness to learn is 0 and to change is 0, your flexibility measure result will be 0 x 0 = 0. If your learning is 5 and your change is 3 then it will be 5 x 3 = 15, and if the learning is 10 and the change is 10, then 10 x 10 = 100.

It is very important to keep this flexibility/teachability measurement in your mind when you are dealing with any new data of information, any experience in your life. It will help you gain the best outcome possible; rigidity and a closed mind will not serve you much.

The bottom line here is this: whenever your flexibility and teachability measurement are lower than 100, you will be cutting yourself short and you will not really learn as you otherwise would and could.

Do or Think?

How many of us want to achieve something in life? There is an old debate on how much we should do and how much we should think. One argument is that actions should be more than thoughts. The other one is the opposite. Another argument is 50% and 50%. Whatever it is, would you like to clarify whether actions or thinking needs to be done more? Let me break them down for you first:

Thinking (the Why): Thoughts, ideas, goals, desires, passion, behavior, motive, energy, mental process, vibration, intention, feelings, emotions, etc.

Actions (the How): Physical actions, activities, setting a plan, actual steps, techniques, strategies, etc.

The chances of you saying, like most people in the world, we should spend more time on the action and doing part, are high. As this supports an idea that we all know – nothing really gets done without action – and that there are *too* many thinkers who never get to the doing part! Which leads us to think that the doing part is the reason makes things happen and we can apply various models to that, which gives more credit to favoring actions. But what I see is that facts are quite the opposite. Let's examine this with a good example. In the corporate world, who gets paid more – the thinker or the doer? The CEO of the company or the hard-working employee at the bottom of the corporate ladder?

This is one of the biggest myths ever sold to us. While rich thinkers are getting even richer, poor people are getting poorer thanks to being fooled with the idea of 'hard work and security.'

The good question now is, what do you think successful, rich people are teaching their kids – to do more or to think more? An even better question for you – what have *you* been focusing on in your life and how far has that brought you? I would say that this is a question of importance that requires your attention, as it holds many answers for you within itself…

Think about it – have you seen *anything* being done or created without thinking or imagining it first? I totally agree that the doing part is a necessary process to bring any thought, any idea to life, but not understanding the full concept will mislead people. Focusing only, or mostly, on the how draws people's attention away from what they want. In fact, nothing will be done and we will not get what we want without the why. They limit themselves with such thoughts as "if I only knew how, I would be rich or successful". In other words, people won't take any step to their real wants 'why' without figuring out the "how" first. To think that you NEED the how first or at all, will keep you from being creative. It drains and paralysis you. And that leads people to settle for less and abandon their dreams.

Let's play a game together here. Say you want to learn a new language. Which way is easier to start learning – to figure out the how or the why? Let's try to ask the 'How' questions and see how easy/difficult to answer them, and then the 'Why' questions and see how easy/difficult to answer those. I want you to ask yourself each and every question of those in the 'how' column and see how many sub-questions will arise and if it is easy or not.

Then I want you to ask yourself the 'Why' question and see how easy/difficult to answer it.

The HOW	The WHY
How I will learn?	Why do I want to learn this language?
How I will find someone to practice with?	
How I can apply it in my life?	
How I will use it?	
How…?	

You may find that the 'How' questions will take much longer time and much greater effort to answer them and will send you to a loop of non-satisfied answers that makes you even more confused about 'How'. The 'Why' questions, on the other hand, you may find, will be answered with more than one answer and guide you to your main purpose and reason for doing what you want to do. That will lead you where you want to be without a single 'How' question. From where I see it, the secret resides in the right questions we ask ourselves.

I would suggest that all you need is to invest in your 'Whys'. Fulfill your desire and soul with possibilities, and I promise you will see wonders, and I also promise you will discover the 'How' on the way during your 'Whys'. You have to dream it, think it, and create it in your mind first. This book that you are reading now, was made literally from 99% of 'Why' and I invested probably 1% on the 'How' part. I didn't know how to start or what I would write, how it would be published, how I would get the money. All my 'Hows' came with almost zero effort. All I had to do was to think it, dream it, and create it in my mind. Where do you think the Burj Khalifa came from?

Failure

The only time you will fail is when you give up on trying. There is nothing called failure, there is only feedback, and a step forward to where you want. FYI, J. K. Rowling, the author of *Harry Potter*, got rejected 12 times as she tried to publish her novel.

<u>There are so many reasons why people fail. To mention a few, people 'fail' because:</u>
- They listen to, and take advice from, the wrong people who don't even have what they want.
- They have low 'teachability measurement'; they are not 'smart enough' to accept change; they are not willing to give up on their old thinking patterns.
- They spend way too much time and effort on discovering the 'How'. Then they worry about details of how their plans can't really happen and how they don't have the means to do it.
- They don't spend enough time on inner work; they don't invest enough on changing their inner worlds. They don't

- even try to install new patterns and aim for any new unconscious competence and awareness.
- They get distracted with their environment and doubt themselves whether they can do it or not.
- They fear judgment, blame, and failure.
- They fear going out of their comfort zone to somewhere unknown.

For you to create the life of your dreams, you have to create a rich and juicy environment *inside*. For seeds to sow, for you to water them and bloom as desired, you will need fertile ground.

You need your mind to be flexible, creative, and supportive, get aligned with nature and the law of attraction around you so you will be in its flow. In order to build Burj Khalifa, you need a strong base, a strong platform.

If you are reading this and are saying, "but I know all this stuff", are you serious? Do you really know it for sure? Then where is the result? Do you have the outcome of what you know?

My dear reader, "to know and not to do, is not to know", said Stephen Covey.

I hope I got you all excited, because I promise you the next chapter will blow your mind and make your jaw drop.

8

YOU ARE FEELING YOUR THOUGHTS

What is the comfort zone?

The word 'comfort' doesn't necessarily mean it is comfortable or good for you.

I would like to start by first giving you an introduction to how we function.

Allow me to go a little deeper and more scientific so you get a logical understanding of the body, mind and your neurology, as some people might think that what I say is some *nonsense bullshit* and what happens to them is pure luck.

The human being is a combination of four different parts: the spiritual being, the physical being, the emotional being, and the mental being.

Chemically speaking, we are made of hydrogen, oxygen, nitrogen, and carbon. These are the same elements that stars are made of. Yet, our natural chemical construction is different from that of the stars.

From a biological perspective, we can downsize our body all the way from the body system, organs, tissues, down to cells. From a physics perspective we can downsize cells all the way from molecules, atoms, subatomic particles, protons, and electrons down to neurons, gluons, quarks, and mesons (electromagnetic vibration waves of light called QUANTA).

Digging deeper into the human body and downsizing it shows that as a scientific measure within an atom is ENERGY. Which means that every single cell of our body is made of vibrating waves called energy. WE ARE ENERGY. You can even go as far as saying that you are made of light.

Everything else in our physical world is made of atoms – your book, chair, car, and anything else physical in this world is also made up of atoms and, therefore, made of energy.

Everything in our physical Universe – including the invisible air that you breathe – is made of atoms and, therefore, made of energy.

You might be wondering now, so what? What am I trying to say? What does that have to do with this 'comfort zone'? Everything will become clear and even more interesting. For now, I want you to remember that everything, including you, constantly vibrates at a frequency and generates energy.

Would you be able to define in your own words what a neurological connection is? Yeah, me neither. But, look at this.

Your Nervous System is capable of making $(10^{10})^{11}$ possible neurological connections. That is the number ten, with ten zeros behind it, written eleven times! This number is so big that we have no conscious idea of what to compare it with. Here's what you want to keep in mind:
- You have more possible neurological connections, even if you are not using them all, than the number of all the stars in our visible Universe.
- You have more possible neurological connections than all the atoms in the entire Universe, according to quantum physicist Dr. Paul Goodwin.

Then, if we have this magnificent possibility and unlimited potential, how do we explain a world of people that struggle to learn new languages, or to achieve their goals, or heal diseases?

For decades, scientists have believed that we only have neurons in our brains. Deepak Chopra, in his book called *Quantum Healing*, published in 1989, proved that neurons are everywhere in the body. In fact, neurotransmitters reside in every single cell of our body. This means that our brain can, and does, communicate with any part of our body constantly. Our thoughts are communicated to all our cells, all the time. This is the first proof in history of the mind-body connection.

Now, that's not only interesting, that is also extremely important for us to know, because that scientifically proves the mind-body connection! The thoughts that we hold in our mind affect our body.

And even before I got introduced to all that knowledge, I used to say, "It is all in your head." The fact is that Deepak Chopra's findings now validate the effect that the mind has on our physical body.

By knowing all this now, we realize that we have the possibilities and opportunities to create new choices by engaging our minds to focus on this potential. So, what new choices do we have and can we create by knowing this? Good question, especially when you have new learning.

The main target here for all of that knowledge is obviously health. With this phenomenal knowledge that we have now, we have the possibility of healing what was not possible for us to be healed before. Your body has this miraculous and incredible power that can rewire, change, rebuild, transform, and heal itself. Of course, only if you do something about it.

Michael Hutchinson's book *Mega Brain*, written in 1986, narrates the story about a medical doctor who had a lifelong friend. His friend lived a completely normal life. He had a job, a family, kids, and a dog. When his friend died, the doctor did the autopsy on his friend. When he cut open his head, he found that there was no brain! Yes, you read that right, no brain! He had what is called 'Hydrocephalus'. The space in the skull for the brain was filled with water instead. This man had no brain since he was born. He had the brain stem, and a very, very thin layer of brain cells, but inside of that was all water-like fluid. But no brain!

You can't help but wonder how this is possible. Based on what we have learnt so far, we can analyze that by saying, in very simple terms, that the functions of the brain were reassigned throughout the whole body. Do you think that this person would have been able to live a normal life if he was told that he didn't have a brain at some point of his life?

There are similar cases around the world, and these cases show not only the adaptability and the resilience of the human brain, but also how little we know about one of our most important organs. It also shows us how powerfully beliefs impact our lives, and how they can affect us.

Remember that you are a joyous, creative expression of life, that you are a magnificent being with the most powerful nervous system that has unlimited potential, a potential beyond measure. All this leads me to believe that EVERYTHING you dream of, is possible for you.

Your powerful organ called the brain

Some facts about it:
- 98% of our knowledge about the human brain has been learned in the last 10 years!
- 80% of everything that scientists knew about the brain by 1990 is today proven to be false!

Hold on a second, didn't it just prove that what we don't know, we don't know? That is an amazing example. It also proves that what we do know, may just as well be proven false as we learn new things.

Until 1990, doctors were taught that our brain is hard-wired. Thanks to modern science and with the new devices developed, we can now monitor the human brain while it is still operational – alive, seeing exactly which part of the brain is involved in which functions. That is how they knew that the brain is not hard-wired! and discovered something called 'brain plasticity', a.k.a. neuroplasticity, which is a term that refers to the brain ability to change and create new neural-pathways – remaps, makes new connections, and retracts the old ones. Brain plasticity includes changes in the neural network resulting from practicing or learning new skill. Without this ability, any brain (including non-human brain), would be unable to develop or recover from injuries.

We have also learned that our thoughts are real! It is not just a thought, it is a material thing, made of energy (bioelectrical and biochemical impulses) and best of all, thoughts are the most compelling and influential energy known to us!

Some brain research facts:
- When 10% dehydrated – it is 50% less efficient!
- It has 160,000 kilometers of blood vessels!
- It is *always* on – it never rests throughout our whole life.
- One brain cell is more complexly and cryptically wired than the entire telephone network of the world.

- It holds 100 billion neurons – as many stars as are in the Universe.
- It is capable of 10,000 Trillion operations per second!
- It is at least 1000 times faster than the fastest supercomputer in the world!
- We were not born hard-wired!
- There is genius ability in each and every one of us.
- We are limitless in our capacity to learn and grow fast.

How we create our reality

What is reality? My favorite part and the least easy pill to swallow. Why? Because it simply shows us how we are responsible for all the things happens 'to us'.

Our reality is formed and filtered by sensory data or information. This information is neutral and entirely meaningless when we receive it in its raw form. Then we start to assign value and meaning to this data. This meaning-making is designed by our model of the world. Then the interaction between our internal reality and our physiology produces the feeling-making state. Then we receive feedback, starting with our behavior, which is a feedback to our feeling- and meaning-making process. The second feedback is our result, which is a feedback from the behavior, and this is how we put our results and feedback into our experience.

Figure 1A **Process of creating our reality.**

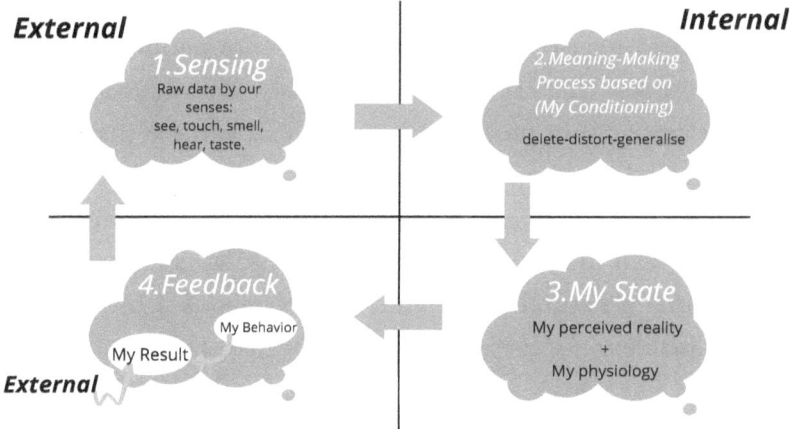

To experience anything, we rely on our five senses. These senses provide us with meaningless data called sensory data. My sensory data, for example from my eyes, will acknowledge my brother, but it will not determine what he means to me, or what I feel about him right now. Sensory data will allow me to experience my brother talking to me, my response, however, will be based on my feeling and meaning processes.

Our five senses are processing approximately four hundred billion (or twenty million as some might say) units of information per second. Regardless of which number is right, it is still a massive number of units for our minds to process per second! So how do we process this information and make some meaning to it? By three data processes: delete, distort, and generalize. When these processes are done, it is reduced to approximately two thousand (if you think it is four hundred billion) or one hundred and thirty (if you think it is twenty million) units of information, so we are able to process this experience consciously. Which means that most of our sensory process is lost. But can you see that this is good news? To know that our reality is limited by the data we receive from our senses and there are things that we might not know of which still do have some effect on us? We are surrounded by all sorts of natural and manmade frequencies. Our eyes are simply unable to see these. One good example of these is wireless networks. Our senses are naturally limited and can't perceive all the available frequencies around us. For instance, as far as our eyes are concerned, we can see only a certain color spectrum and that's it. Yet, animals and machines can see much more… And that gives you an opportunity to change the way you see things, which will significantly change your perception about life.

We delete the data that doesn't matter to us or doesn't sit right with what we know and believe, and so we relate to and feel a sense of familiarity with what does matter to us.

Distortion is recognizing the information, whether it is bad or good. All experiences go into categories determined by our preferences that are characteristic of us and our value and belief systems.

Then we generalize. Let me give an example for this. When someone generalizes and says, "My spouse never listens to me," how much effort do you think this person will put in a conversation when in communication with their spouse? I would say not much as their logic would say no point in putting too much effort in communicating with someone who doesn't listen. We only produce behaviors that support what we believe to be true. Having said that, it gives you a brief peek into why and how people behave and think differently. Sometimes we fall apart when communicating with each other and mostly with ourselves.

When it comes to the feeling-making process, we talk about our emotions. Emotion is what fuels us for action. I haven't – yet – seen anyone who achieved anything without being emotionally charged about that achievement. For a more technical explanation, emotion is experienced when a certain chemical is produced in our blood. That's why prescribed medicine is often mood-related, the medicine is designed to impact your chemical state or balance so it can change your mood. There are three ways to change your mood: physically alter or convert your chemical status (food, drugs, alcohol, etc.), or by dance, exercise, sex, massage, etc., or change your meaning-making process.

Then the feedback, which sums up and combines everything that has happened inside and outside of us as a result of our meaning-and-feeling making process. Feedback includes the responses and reactions we get, which is basically our behavior and our result.

Starting with the **behavior,** is all the activities of the mind (conscious and unconscious) which we are mostly well aware of with reference to our result. Changing our behavior will produce a different result.

Let me give you an example here so you can relate. Let's say my red car is parked outside the restaurant and someone just rushes into the restaurant and loudly says, "Whose red car is parked outside? Someone just crashed into it." I will instantly imagine that this is *my* car (meaning-making process). I will start to feel scared and angry, an adrenaline rush will take place and a chemical flow will begin all over my body (feeling-making process). And I will furiously run outside to see what is happening (my behavior). This may lead into an argument or a fight, based on the whole process I associated with the red car (my result). But what if I just came out and I realized that this wasn't my car, how would that change my whole physiology and what would it do to the adrenaline rush in my body? You get it? OK, great.

We all have some **results** in our lives – from our relationships, job, bank account, our own health, or basically anything else. Whether it is good results or bad ones, however you look at it, you would agree that you are the one who created them with your behavior. Your thoughts, actions, and feelings are the very thing that has brought you to where you are today. We tend to have many excuses and complaints about how our lives didn't work the way we wanted them to. But to look at it in a more realistic way, it is us at the end of the day who did or did not do certain things that affected the results in our lives.

It is crucial to evaluate the outputs we produce in our life and have real meaningful clarity on how we impact these results we produce and where they come from in the first place. Learning these qualities is the key to continuous success in all aspects of our life.

If it is the behavior that affected the result, then what caused the behavior itself? We know well that it is the emotional and mental **state** that determines our behavior. We can't produce resourceful behavior, for example, if we are in an unresourceful state like in the previous example. We cannot even think intelligently or intellectually while in distress – emotional or otherwise.

We ask again: what it is causing our state? This is where things get a bit complicated, as there are a variety of factors that influence our state automatically. We can put them all under the label **conditioning.** Between the ages of 0 and 7 is when our dominant unconscious mind gets formed. In those years, it is like a sponge, absorbing everything around it, and believes it as its reality. The rational mind during this time is not interfering or rationalizing anything. These are the years of processing and creating our beliefs and emotions and this is the sum total of all our past experiences, learnings, memories, beliefs, values about ourselves and the world around us, our acquired characteristics character, our attitudes, etc. Our mind uses these specific filters as a reference for the process of creating our reality. Our adult mind will filter the information and data that it receives according to our childhood conditioning.

So for us to change any result in our life we will need to look at the root cause of the problem, which is always one or more of our filters within our conditioning. And until this happens and we break this cycle and pattern of behaviors, nothing will change from our results in life.

Let's explore some facts about the unconscious mind:
- It controls up to 95% or more of our perception and behavior and records everything.
- It averages 10 billion actions per second!
- It sees in pictures and patterns.
- It doesn't know time (no past or future).
- It can't tell real from imagined or truth from a lie – whatever you tell it or send it in an image or picture form, it believes to be absolutely true. It is not logical, it is the feeling mind.
- It works in an orderly manner.

Our Reticular Activation System (RAS) processes these four hundred billion or twenty million pieces of information, deleting, distorting and generalizing it down to two thousand or one hundred and twenty. It forms part of your conditioned mind and functions up to 800 times faster than your conscious mind. Every sensory impulse received will literally go through it first, where it decides whether the information received is important to you or not. It will pass the information to your conscious mind *only* if it is entitled to be on the priority list. For example, if the impulse received is the sound of an alarm siren, it will instantly prioritize it for you, passing this information to your conscious mind, grabbing your attention regardless of what you are busy with at the time. This happens because the alarm sound is on your priority list, as a result of your mind being conditioned to act when hearing a siren.

This means that you need to learn to upload what is really important to you, to your RAS. This is exactly why when you concentrate much of your attention on problems, like toxic or unhealthy relationships, all your RAS can bring to your attention is more of what you have stressed as important to it. If you worry about attracting toxic people and relationships in your life, it will impress itself to your priority list and your RAS will do whatever it can, to bring more of it to your attention. It will see toxic relationships as a priority to you as you are focusing so much on them.

That finally brings us to the juicy part that explains the comfort zone.

Psycho-Cybernetic Mechanism "Maxwell Maltz"

Before I explain the Psycho-Cybernetic Mechanism, first let me explain the Cybernetic Mechanism that we find in some machines and animals. This mechanism is a control and response mechanism. We use it everywhere nowadays, like in autopilot systems or air conditioning systems, for example.

The Cybernetic Mechanism is been designed to monitor a certain limits or measurements and take action to correct any divergence or changes. Air conditioners now have climate control and are able to maintain a set temperature by adjusting the settings of the air conditioner to recompense with any other influences that affect the temperature. The air conditioner will activate and deactivate to maintain the set temperature because of the cybernetic mechanism. Autopilot technology in aircraft also uses the cybernetic mechanisms.

The Psycho-Cybernetic Mechanism monitors what we refer to as your comfort zone.

The Psycho-Cybernetic Mechanism is in charge of keeping you in your comfort zone (safe), no matter how badly you want to change. When it picks up any divergence from your comfort zone, it sends feedback to your nervous system which then tries to 'correct' that divergence by creating an emotional alarm or motive to bring you back into your comfort zone.

Let's say a single person enjoys their single life, the non-committed lifestyle, and the variety of options available, yet wants to settle down and be in a healthy relationship. Logically, it will require more commitment and sacrificing the variety and the lifestyle. In return, this person will have stability, true happiness, real love, care, and the possibility of building a beautiful family.

At this point their Psycho-Cybernetic Mechanism would kick in and send signals to cause doubts, fear, and anxiety. It will cause this person to rationalize things and start to think twice about being in a committed relationship. Please bear in mind that this happens automatically and so fast that you have no idea that it is happening at all. It will start justifying old behaviors. The individual might find it perfectly reasonable to take a break since they have been in a relationship for some time. The mechanism will literally find dozens of excuses as to why they should take a break and why the relationship isn't working. All this is to bring the individual back to their old, 'safe' comfort zone.

The mechanism doesn't even know if you are happy or unhappy in your comfort zone. Its job is to simply keep bringing you back into your comfort zone.

This is a very critical point and can be applied on pretty much everything in your life. You want to change but you feel that you can't. It can be applied for positive things as well, sometimes extra money in your pocket is out of your comfort zone and doesn't feel safe!

Without resetting this system, nothing will change! This system causes you to consistently behave the way you do and will continue to keep bringing you back to your old ways of being.

I hope that your jaw has dropped already, and I got you excited to know how to reset your Psycho-Cybernetic Mechanism!

Virginia Satir said: "Familiarity is the most powerful force in human beings." The opposite of familiarity is the unknown. When you were a child, almost everything was unknown. Yet, as a child, each day brought new exploration and a new set of possibilities. When you learned to walk, you kept going even if you fell, you got back up each time, over and over. You kept doing this because of your unshakable desire and belief that you would walk. I haven't seen, heard or experienced a child giving up on walking because of falling down! I've never heard a child saying, "That's it for me, I have fallen a hundred times, it seems that walking is not my thing!"

The Amygdala

The amygdala (a tiny, pea-sized membrane in the limbic part of our brain), has tremendous power over your perceptions and actions. Its job is to pick up any divergence from your comfort zone. It senses potential and real stress and then orders the release of stress hormones. This causes you to have doubts, fear, or anxiety.

The amygdala is a very valuable mechanism that we have. It is there to warn you and save your life. It stops you from doing what you were doing, urges questions like: "Hey, watch out! What are you doing? Are you sure you want to carry on?" That is great when we are being protected from real, actual danger.

Most of us always respond to the amygdala's signals by simply stepping back into our comfort zone. The benefit in learning to manage, assess, and take control of our response to the amygdala is very resourceful. It would be most beneficial if we are able to respond to the amygdala with clarifying questions before taking any action. If you are going to create the life you want and achieve your goals, you need to be able to step out of your comfort zone, not 99% but 100% out of your comfort zone and stay out there.

I want you to understand that all of these systems are really part of you, and they are designed to serve you, not to work against you. In order for you to make them serve you well, you need to understand and learn as much as you can about these systems. Once you do, they will serve you, your current dreams and desires at their best instead of you having no choice apart from just reacting the way you always have.

9

E-MOTION

What is E-motion?

We know by now that the unconscious mind is the emotional part of you, and emotions play a great part in conditioning your mind. It is a chemical and protein reaction that is released from the brain whenever you experience a significant event or emotion. Your mind will react by releasing those chemicals together with sending neurons down the newly created neural-pathways. This is how we create a strong belief in an instant. That process happens in seconds. A perfect example for this is when we experience great fear or a near-death experience and a new belief is created almost instantaneously.

Imagine being bitten by a spider! You'll see the spider biting you, you will feel enormous pain at the same time and you will know, based on your old conditioning, that you may die if it is a poisoned one. This experience will be imprinted in your mind in a matter of seconds and you will be forever scared of a spider when you see one.

Experiencing a similar environment will fire the same neural-pathways and will trigger and release the stress hormones that will remind you of your past experience.

Neurons that fire together – wire together

Emotions when intense enough always produce various behaviors. They can serve us extremely well when we are in control of them. Your emotions will support you in creating the life you want. Unfortunately, most people hold onto a massive bulk of unprocessed negative emotions, to the extent that it becomes such a burden that it affects all their focus, thinking, and behavior, producing identical results in their life. We project our problems and behaviors on others and blame them for not coping with our drama, instead of changing the behavior that causes any type of conflict. It is a custom in Western society to say things like: "You have to accept me for who I really am! If you really love me, you will accept me with all my flaws." And so on.

Another presupposition states: "People are not their behavior." People can change **only** if they want to and have the resources to do so. I am sure that my behavior has changed throughout my life. I am also sure that I'm still the same person. The question here is what resources are needed and what behavior needs to change.

Emotions play a big role in our lives, even and especially from the health perspective! Positive emotions are great for our body. For example, what happens when you are experiencing any positive excitement or any form of happiness? Your whole body goes into the feeling-good state of emotions and your unconscious mind instantly starts processing good emotions. Every cell of your body will start dancing and glowing, and you'll have huge amounts of energy flowing through your body.

You'll be surprised to know that most people are not aware of that that negative emotions are not good for the body. In fact, unprocessed negative emotions are the biggest cause of all our diseases! 90% of our diseases, which literally means 'lack of ease', and all dark and degenerative diseases are caused by either a significant emotional event, or by piled up unprocessed negative emotions.

The biggest and major negative emotions since ancient times are anger, sadness, fear, hurt, and guilt. Your mind will keep them unprocessed in your body, until it gets some sort of learning or resolution to process them.

Emotions tend to build up and, in turn, we tend to push them away, as we've been taught to resist things that don't make us feel good. Instead of *feeling* the things that don't feel good, we start looking for answers. But the thing is that answers are not in the outside world, they are inside of us, because the feelings are from inside of us. We call them trapped emotional patterns and we experience them that way. If it is an experience we have not completed and come back to the self after, we do find one way or another to keep repeating these patterns of experiences. We traumatize ourselves, we pick partners, and we create the same emotional dynamic, the same physiological disability, because our energy is not flowing! One of the greatest discoveries is that 90% of our energy is used to suppress energy from the past.

We have this old debate that says big boys don't cry or men should not show that they are weak, or when a child cries, we shush them and tell them not to cry, etc. Our problem is not the negative emotions. Negative emotions must exist in our life at certain time for us to appreciate the positive ones. It is a pathway for our growth and wisdom, we can't really reach to certain learning or wisdom without the lesson itself, of course. But the real problem is when we suppress them inside our body.

E-Motion literally means energy-in-motion or moving. We *need* to move this energy. Where do you think the energy will go if you suppress or keep them inside your body?

Have you ever noticed that when your head aches and you focus on the head aching itself it gets worse? What we learned from the Western medicine is to just take the pill and then you are cured. What this does is something called a neurotoxin. What it does do is just block the electric signal that your body is trying to send to you. Whenever you have a pain in your body, it is your body way of telling you, "Ouch, it hurts, STOP IT! Take care of me." When you want to get to know the cause, ask yourself what is the negative source, what is the negative emotion? De-tox it, clear it. Western medicine, the elephant in the living room as they say, controls all health-related issues, and doctors encourage people to take prescribed medicines or drugs. It is by no small coincidence that tens of billions of dollars are made in profits by Western medicine. I'm not saying that all medicines are all not necessary., But what we are missing out completely is that when people are in pain, we give them some drug for that pain to be suppressed; when people have some disease, we give them medicines to suppress the symptoms of that disease, when in reality those symptoms are the body crying out, begging, for attention, telling us there is something wrong here. Know this, the biggest single imbalance that we suffer from is emotional baggage, our trapped emotional baggage. Our body has the resilient and innate ability to heal itself without the constant need of these prescribed drugs. It is proven scientifically that the power of our mind can heal our body over and over again. The *placebo effect* proves that the mind can heal itself whether it is a sugar pill or a fake operation. The *nocebo effect*, on the other hand, shows how even when people get the right drug, if their mind tells them they cannot be cured, they don't heal.

We are living in the most toxic time on the planet. We are flooded with and surrounded by metal toxicity, heavy metal, chemicals, and pesticides that are spread in our food and environment. If negative emotions are in your cells, they will almost be blocking your toxicity in!

We are addicted to our emotions. The same negative emotions that go outside of you, go inside of you as well. Your blood is pumping these chemicals of negative emotions. Your cells have these protein receptors that bind these molecules of emotions. Here comes the big one: the interesting part about these receptors is that they are the same receptors our body produced when taking heroin or any drugs. And what do you call a heroin consumer? An addict, right? We are addicted to our emotions.

> *"The first step to success is to think of what*
> *you want, not what you don't want,*
> *if you keep doing what you are doing,*
> *you are going to get what you are getting."*
>
> —Raymon Grace.

Our body is waiting for that magical moment when we begin to allow ourselves to come out of the survival mode and begin to be able to open up and become vulnerable to feeling again. This is the first step of healing our heart and getting back to our state of joy, because this is who we really are. When we see someone happy, we tend to ask, "What is wrong with them, are they drunk or something?" while they are really in their natural state.

Survival State

Where does this stress come from, have you wondered? Stress is an emotional tension resulting from highly demanding events or circumstances. We tend to create this state of emotional tension when we can't predict the outcome of certain events or situations, when we feel that we are out of or losing control over things, or when we feel a certain threat, danger, or fear that something is about to get worse in our lives.

According to Dr. Joe Dispenza, a great neuroscientist, author and researcher, there are three types of stress. Physical (born of accidents, injuries, health, etc.), chemical (virus, bacteria, etc.), and emotional (born of tragedy, debts, traffic jam, break-ups, etc.).

All of these types of stress create an imbalance in the body, as the stress response is what the body does innately to bring itself back to normal. Once the body senses danger, it will activate its nervous system (fight or flight response). The body will start to gain as much energy as it can from all its resources so as to adapt to the stressful environment.

It is an absolutely incredible system that all organisms have to protect themselves from danger. However, this system is beneficial when it is been used, right. All organisms can tolerate this system for only a short period of time. Whether it is a zebra or a gazelle being chased by a lion, once that organism senses danger it instantly switches on the emergency system. The survival mode is switched on in the brain and there is a rush of adrenaline throughout the body. And when what is called the sympathetic nervous system switches on, our pupils dilate, our salivary juices shut down, our heart rate increases, our digestive system shuts down, our respiratory rate increases, blood is sent to the extremities, and the internal system shuts down. It is not the time to relax or think of food or sex or sleep. It is the time to either run, hide, or fight. Amazing system, right? Now, the only difference here between us and the zebra is, once the zebra outruns the lion, a few minutes later, their nervous system starts to get back to normal, their stress response switches off and the body starts to balance itself again. The body needs to rest and repair after such an event in order to get back to normal. It need to recharge its energy again and conserve it for the future.

But, my dear human, you are a slightly different being from the gazelle, right? So, what if you get chased by a lion then? Well, your body will behave and respond similar to the other organisms. It will switch on its nervous system and start to run, hide from (hopefully not fight) the predator, and that will be super adaptable and doable by the nervous system, right? Great. But what if that lion is outside your house and waiting for you to come out? That will keep the stress response extended and your sympathetic nervous system switched on for longer, won't it? Then this is not a short period of time (which we can tolerate) the system is switched on for anymore. No organism can live in emergency mode for an extended period of time. Now, of course there is no lion outside your house. The lion (the predator) in this case, that awaits you outside your house is your boss, co-worker, mother-in-law, or debt collector. What was once highly adaptive becomes maladaptive because their presence is connected to the brain with some sort of feelings that turns on the stress response. The longer you stay in that state, before you know it, you will be heading to what we call disease. If you keep constantly exhausting and mobilizing your energy for some threat or danger out there, then there is no energy left for your inner world to rest, repair, grow, and create.

If you constantly operate your life from a state of stress, you become conditioned to that state of hyperarousal caused by the rush of chemicals. Over time, you will begin to use the problems and conditions in your lives to reaffirm your conditioning or your addiction to that emotion. We become so deeply conditioned to those emotions, just like a drug addict, remember? We need the poor relationship, we need the bad job, we need the abusive people in our life, we need that debt, we need those difficult events in our lives to keep getting that rush of adrenaline, that rush of emotion, and that results in people become addicted to a life that they don't even like.

The interesting part is that when you start to think about your problems, stress release will get activated just by thinking of those problems! Which means that your thoughts could literally make you sick!

As I mentioned earlier, so many diseases around the world are created by the immune system being suppressed – everything from cancer, lupus, food allergy, rheumatoid arthritis and much more – all that is because the immune system is compromised.

Trading negative emotions (anger, sadness, guilt, jealousy, hurt, competition, etc.) for elevated emotions (joy, love, compassion, care, gratitude, trust, acceptance, etc.) ten minutes a day opens your heart to those emotions and allows them to take a place in your inner world. Your stress hormones go down and your immune system gets upregulated to a great level.

When you are chased by a predator, all your attention is drawn to the outer world – where you need to hide, how you will get there, what you need to do. When you are under the effect of those chemicals, you will be thinking about time – how much time does the predator have to get there? How much time do you have to save yourself and 'survive'?

Body, Environment, Time
Now knowing all of that, do you see how our thoughts could literally affect our energy field? Once our body is under the influence of these hormones and chemicals of stress, it starts to draw from the vital invisible energy field surrounding the body and use it to make those chemicals. That energy field will then shrink and we will become more matter and less energy; more particles and less wave. In other words, the more our focus is on the things we are stressed about, the more we narrow our focus on objects, threat and danger; more materialistic than spiritual. This is when people start to get greedy or invidious. "I need to survive," "There is not enough for everyone," etc. Staying in that state and feeling altered from that chemical release will create it as a habit. In fact, it has been said that if the survival mode is on, you will innately think that it is not the time to sit down and create something because you are a prey! Isn't that insane?! Yet, it makes total sense if we take a closer look to it and see what we are doing to our miraculous body and nervous system.

Now we come to a very interesting part. Do you happen to be, or know, someone who always think of the worst-case scenario, so when it does happen, they don't get disappointed or surprised or sad? Do you remember that the subconscious mind/unconscious mind works in pictures and patterns? It doesn't work with words directly, hence, it doesn't process negatives directly. So, whenever you are speaking, feeling, listening, your mind will have a series of pictures and start to draw meaning from them. For example, if I say to you, "Don't imagine a blue elephant!", the communication I have left for you after the negating words is the blue elephant. Your mind completely deletes that "don't" word. You need to think about something first in order to not to think about it. But too late, buddy! You already thought of that blue elephant by just processing the words. Whenever you are telling yourself what you don't want in life, your mind has nothing else but a focus on the image of that which you don't want, and that is what manifests. This is exactly what happens when people are living with any sort of emotions. The more they put their focus and attention on a matter, the more they feel and experience separation from everyone and everything. Think about it, it is survival mode, right? The more you are in that mode, the more you would become selfish, thinking only of how you will survive, the less giving, less vulnerable, less caring, and disconnected, right? Now, what happens if the stress is created by the feeling of losing control, or that you can't control everything in your life, that you can't predict the future, or worse, predict the worst-case scenario, or something or someone is causing things to get worse in your life? When you live on a daily basis with that kind of hormone release, you will begin to feel the need to control everything in your life. When you feel a loss of control, you will try to predict the next moment that is based on your memories of the past.

Which means that people under stress are craving the known, trying to get back to the familiarity in their lives, because in survival, the unknown is a terrifying place! So they begin to shift their attention from one problem to another, one person to another, one thing to another, one place to another, and so on. When this happens, because every thought and element has a neurological network in the brain and creates an arousal of those chemicals, it starts to create different circuits in the brain going to different directions. It creates an imbalance and that results in the brain functioning in a very incoherent state. The arousal of those chemicals drives the brain to a highly analytical state or over-focused state, thinking over and over again about the same problem. Now, when your focus is narrowed, you think of the worst-case scenario. Why? Because in survival if you prepare for the worst, and what happens is less than that, you have a better chance of surviving. This is where people spend most of their life – thinking of when they will be in that stress state. It turns out, according to some studies, that most people are living in survival mode 70% of the time.

When we allow the chemicals or emotions to last for few hours or days, we experience what they call a mood, or being moody. If we allow the same emotions for weeks or months, it will be called temperament, like when someone has a 'temper'. And if we keep it for years, that will be called personality traits. And here is how and where most people's personalities are defined by their experiences from the past.

So, now you understand that stress is when the body is knocked or kicked out of balance and that the stress hormone pushes your genetic buttons and creates disease in the body.

Hopefully this knowledge begs the question, is there anyone or anything worth living in that shitty state?

It is said that someone with good health has a thousand wishes, and without it they have one. I heard the story of a lady, whose husband called her and shared great wisdom just before he passed away. He asked her to come close, and said, "I want to tell you something, now listen very carefully. I have not much strength now; I can only say this once." She said, "I'm listening, darling, what is it?" He said, "Remember this each morning: the moment you take your head off the pillow, you have all you need."

10

CONCLUSION & CLOSURE

By now, after all the stories and facts I have shared with you, I'm hoping that you have got a clear image about the life that we didn't know happens within us.

We are now at that point that will guide you on how to use this information to communicate with yourself and others.

> *The most beautiful people on Mother Earth are made of the ugliest moments in their lives.*

Remember that you are responsible for what happened, is happening, and will happen to you. You may ask how you are responsible for the abuse that happened to you at a young age, for example. My answer will be: I refuse to give anyone or anything power over me. I refuse to play the role of victim. Yes, I have been sexually, physically, verbally, and emotionally abused since the age of four or five. I didn't want it. But the fear state that I was living in brought even more of what I was focused on. I now know that I somehow attracted all that into my life in order for me to learn the lesson and become who I am at that moment. To reframe all that: I'm grateful and so proud of myself to have experienced all that and still stand tall. How could I be writing about these experiences, reach where I am, achieve this state of gratitude and unconditional love, and be capable of helping others heal without me feeling and knowing all of what I have witnessed?

Remember, without pain and suffering we will not move forward. Better said: we grow through our suffering. It is normal. Life will happen for us as long as we are growing and moving through it. A caterpillar does not become a butterfly unless it goes through the process of growth.

Let me share another perspective. Did you know that the eagle has the longest lifespan amongst all birds – about 70 years? In order to live that long, the eagle must take a hard decision. In its forties, its long and flexible talons can no longer grab its prey and its long and sharp beak becomes bent. Its aged, heavy wings become stuck to its chest and makes it difficult for it to fly. Then the eagle is left with only two options – die or go through a painful process which lasts 120 days.

The process requires that the eagle flies to a mountain top and first knocks out its beak against a rock and waits for it to grow. Then it pulls its talons and feathers and waits for them to regrow! After five months, the eagle takes its famous flight of rebirth and lives for another 30 years. This is a very interesting myth about the eagle's life and metaphorical story that shows us that we need to be willing to change in order to grow and survive. Another thing we can learn from the eagle is how to manage challenges. When there is a storm, most birds head for shelter, but the eagle is the only bird that starts flying above the cloud, taking advantage of the heavy and stormy winds to avoid the rain. If we want to allow in new opportunities and enjoy the present moment instead of dwelling on the past, we must get rid of our old selves and stop pointing fingers and say, "*You* did this to me." We are all looking for happiness, each and every one of us, in one form or another. We have had to suffer and feel the pain at some level in order for us to recognize and appreciate the happy moments. Make happiness your default emotional state of mind. Go cry, hustle and bustle, and then get back to your default emotional state of happiness. Our brain is set for survival, not to make us happy and that is why it kicks us back to the comfort zone the moment we want to change. If we get used to a certain financial state where we don't have a good relationship with money or we are not used to having extra money, for example, and then our income starts to increase, our comfort mechanism will kick us straight back to our old status, even though the new one makes us happier. Remember the Psycho-Cybernetic Mechanism? That's right!

"Yesterday I was clever, so I wanted to change the world. Today I'm wise, so I'm changing myself."

—Rumi

Time heals everything

This is an absolute bullshit statement and not even to be considered. Time does nothing if you don't work on yourself and don't let go of the attached negative emotions. Time lets things cook inside you, suppresses things, and keeps it there. And at some point, later on, it will bring you a baked event from what you didn't let go of. Similar pattern(s), different faces or events.

The actress in me

Since I was little, I wanted to travel the world and become an actress, remember? However, I never took an acting class, nor did I go online to search the requirements to become one. I had a lot of friends back home who were actors, directors, and scenarists, but again, I didn't have the urge to go for it when they asked me how come I was not an actress! My reply or "excuse" was, "I want to be an actress in Hollywood, not here! I *know* that I don't need acting classes, it is in my innate ability, put me in front of a camera and that's all you need to do." I did model once in my life. But again, I was not passionate about it – with full respect to all the models around the world, I just felt that it was not what I'm here for, I have different purpose than posing! It just didn't sit right with me, even though I was really good at it. I kept searching for what I want, and what is my purpose until I found my way. It is the new knowledge and healing methods and this journey that I'm on and will keep discovering until the moment I leave the planet in a physical form.

You see, I wanted to become an actress to show the world that I matter, I exist, I'm beautiful, and wanted them to look at me and give me some attention. But after this part of me that seeks false external validation has been healed, I don't have to try to show up and exist for people to acknowledge me and recognize me! Of course, external appreciation, feedback, and opinions (but not validation) matter when it is from the right people – family members we trust, good friends we have, a loving partner we care for. All these opinions – from an opinion about a dress to wear to a career or life-changing decisions – and feedback are healthy when we want them for the right purpose.

The reason why I got drawn on to that path is because it has all my passion and compassion, and supports living a life with purpose. The moment I help someone get rid of their pain in a few seconds or a couple of minutes, I feel alive. I feed myself on that feeling and it makes me want and crave even more of it. Seeing someone get rid of their tumor over a lunch break is all that I need to witness for the rest of my life! Witness people heal – and this is how I found my passion and purpose.

Gratitude

It is the most elegant and one of the highest vibrational emotions that anyone could operate from. It has a profound result in all the areas of your life. Being grateful for what you have brings happiness, calmness, and fulfillment in each and every cell of your body. It opens opportunities and healing channels throughout your daily life, it makes you stay in autopilot of happy emotions, and most importantly, it gives you patience when rough times come and allows you to see things from different angle. It allows you to reframe any hardship and cruel events with wisdom and an open heart. It opens our sentience to love and compassion, to care and appreciation.

Once you master gratitude, reframing events and situations will become effortless. My last breakup was painful for me, especially because I had been cheated on and been unappreciated, but just because of the gratitude that I have in my heart, I was able to reframe things and be thankful for what happened and why it happened. It allowed me to forgive and move on. I'm not saying the pain and hurt wasn't there; no, of course, it was there. I felt it and doubted myself; I cried and felt the loss and the rejection as well, but just because of gratitude, I looked at things differently. I thanked that person for coming into my life, and helping me see that his cheating on me had nothing to do with me or my value. I was able to say, "Who knows why this breakup happened. It probably opened a door or two for me that I can't see. My next relationship will be exactly as I want it to be because of the healing and the learnings that I had along the way." It allowed me to experience, for the first time in my life, staying alone without the usual distractions and be as content and happy as I am. And look at me now! Finding my purpose in life, mixing it with my passion. If I continued to be in that relationship, I would not be one-third of how happy I am at this moment.

I could give you hundreds of examples about gratitude, but to wrap it up, what I can say is this: instead of being greedy and ungrateful or always looking for something better than what you have or what others have and not appreciating the present moment, be thankful and grateful for what you do have. Enjoy and appreciate the little things, the cup of coffee you have, the breath you take, the house you live in, the food in your fridge, etc.

I can literally write a whole book about gratitude and things to be grateful for. Stop looking at what others have that you don't. Look for prosperity and growth, instead of looking for something better just for the sake of getting something new. Having said that, there is a huge difference between growth/evolving, and lack of appreciation/being greedy. Growth could be aiming for a more fulfilling career, moving to a more comfortable home, buying a more efficient car, or starting a new, more loving relationship because your awareness of yourself, your being, your challenges, or your desires has shifted. You are no longer doing it to outdo someone else, or do these things to compete with another. You are looking for and creating growth for your own – and others' – happiness, and not greed. Do remember, everything will become so much more enjoyable if you are able to desire for something and, even before you get it, already express gratitude for it as if you already have it! And once you do have that something new, something you desired in your life, you are able to enjoy it in the present moment rather than wishing for 'the next better' thing or version. In order to appreciate our life, we need to appreciate our present as it is the only actual thing we have now, and from that place we can create our beautiful and shiny future. So many rich, famous, and powerful people who seem to have it all are undergoing therapy and using anti-depression pills – if they haven't committed suicide already – as they are not happy, they are not filling their heart and soul with gratitude for what they have and are unable to enjoy the present moment. Which shows that money, fame or even power cannot really buy happiness if we are not feeling it internally.

Contribution

The more you give, the more you receive; the more you take from life, the more life will take from you. It is very well-known rule. In fact, in Islam, it is one of the five pillars in order to become Muslim; it is *that* vital in Islam. This is one of the best blessings that you could have and adopt as a habit. You can contribute with anything that could serve the world and make it a better place. Contribute with time, effort, information, knowledge, money, clothes, donations to foundations and organizations (recycle plastic, feed the poor, help the homeless, help disabled humans or animals, etc.) – the list goes on. The moment you operate from scarcity and a fearful state, or the moment you begin to do things like stealing time or try to rob others of respect, or perhaps steal someone from a relationship, you are saying to the Universe, "I don't really deserve the good in life, I have to sneak around and take it." Become aware of your thoughts of scarcity and beliefs that may be blocking your way to wealth. Then change those beliefs and begin to create new, abundant, and prosperous thinking.

Wealth

Most of us are unaware of the real meaning of wealth. Once we hear the word wealth, we usually tend to think of financial wealth. I invite you to look at wealth as holistic wealth – which means wealth in all areas of our lives – spiritual, physical, mental, emotional, health, family, money, and career. I want you to know, understand, and believe that it is our birthright to be fulfilled in each and every area of your lives, so claim that birthright. Start with wealthy thoughts that serve you best, instead of scarce and self-criticizing thoughts.

Where your focus goes, your energy flows

Here is some guidance to follow throughout your life so you can have peace of mind:

- *Stop worrying about things that you can't control.* Being grumpy about a rainy day won't stop the rain. Enjoying the rain will give the day different taste and value.
- *Stop judging and criticizing yourself.* Most of the time we do it without even realizing it. We tend to be our own worst critic. We wouldn't talk to our friends the way we would to ourselves! Saying things like "I'm shy", "I'm stupid", "I don't deserve better than this", "I will not make it", "I'm chubby or fat", "My skin is horrible", "My hair is awful", "I attract the wrong people into my life", or, worst of all, "I'm not good enough". Remember that you are doing the best you can with the learning and knowledge you have. But if you self-criticize or judge yourself or if you wait until you get that new job, or until you lose weight, or until someone else loves you, you will be denying your existence right now! You are already the perfect outer expression of your 'self' and you will change.

So be kind to yourself and speak nicely, politely, and gently to it as if you're talking to your most beloved ones. Because the changes you will do while loving yourself will always be positive. Always!

- ***Change.*** According to the latest scientific study of creating a new habit and to change a habit, it takes between 18 days to 254 days. For the majority of people involved in that research, it took them more than 60 days. So, basically, it will take you anywhere between two to eight months of daily repetition to apply a new habit. Remember that our mind works with repetition in order to function at its best. So, give yourself the time to change, go easy on yourself. Healing and change take time. It is like onion layers that we peel off. Or like a house to clean. When you start to clean your house, you start with one room at a time, and eventually the whole house is clean. For your mind, start with your thoughts. Your thoughts determine the quality of your life. I know, I know, it is almost impossible to control the roughly 60-70 thousand thoughts we have per day. But thanks to our emotions that make us FEEL the quality of our thoughts, we can change them. How? Once you feel negative emotional charge with a particular thought, acknowledge it, then change it. Become aware of the type of thoughts running through your head and what they make you feel, acknowledge them, then gently and with care, shift your thoughts to what you want and bring them to the present moment. You can change the blueprint of your whole life just by changing your thoughts. What are you going to lose? Nothing, I promise. You have been living your life the way you did so far. If it hasn't served you well and you haven't reach where you wanted to, try and start to change. You are so worth it.

- ***Be authentic, be yourself.*** Be true to yourself and others. We tend to do or don't do things to please others. We fear being judged and criticized, so we stop doing things we like. While it makes us feel 'safe' thanks to not being judged or to not losing someone, we forget who we are and, over age and time, we lose pieces of our authentic self. We then feel lost without a clear image of who we really are and what really makes us happy. We start to have a fragile and weak personality and character, or become rigid and stubborn to any foreign/new idea or belief, because of the fear of our environment and society, and we end up becoming a people-pleaser. Stop for a moment and ask yourself this question: For whom am I doing what I am doing? Honestly answer yourself and consider what your life is revolving around.
- ***Never lose the child in you.*** This is more powerful and several degrees more difficult than you think. By losing pieces of ourselves bit by bit, we lose the child in us, and that's why when we enter a room full of children, we become like kids ourselves. With children, we don't care about what we look like or how we talk or how we are

sitting down, how we laugh or dance, because we know that they are not judging us or gossiping about us. In fact, even if they laugh at us, we take it as a complement. Why? Because to make them happy or smile, we bring the trapped child inside of us out and start to play!

- Sadly enough, our society makes us forget about this joy. We don't want to be pointed at or laughed at or be judged by others. I often get asked while I'm with people how old I am, and they get surprised when they know that we are the same age or that I am even older. I never lost the child in me. I cry when I want, I smile when I feel like it, I dance, run, fall, and laugh at myself, I remember once I dressed up oddly at one of the biggest and most famous malls in the world. Everyone turned to look at me, and I mean everyone! Different cultures, genders, and nationalities. I was laughing, having fun and generally very happy with being myself, not focused at all on the attention (which was largely finger-pointing and ridicule). And I didn't really care how people looked at or thought of me. My ex was walking with me that day, and later on, when he was telling me that he lost interest, he told me that walking next to him that day with that outfit embarrassed him. A week later, one of my friends sent me a picture of a model in Vogue magazine wearing the same exact style! It may not turn out that way all the time, but I promise you, the less you care about how people will think, the more playful and joyous your life will be. You will, as a bonus, attract people in your life with the same level of energy and authenticity as you.

- ***Rejection.*** When it comes to me being happy, no one can stop me. I could stand and dance in a middle of restaurant that has neither a dance floor nor anyone else dancing. I could dance in the middle of the aisles of a grocery store or even in the street. I use dancing as part of my coaching to improve the physical, emotional, and mental state of my clients and for them to embrace their body and accept and believe in themselves exactly how they are. When I like someone, I ask them out. When I was a teenager, I used to sing to a stranger if I thought they looked cute, or asked a stranger on the street to sing for me, or run a race with me. I got rejected quite a few times, to be honest. Even when I tried to be friends with someone, I received rejections. However, that didn't stop me. I always complimented myself about my confidence and the guts to do such things. I have never cared about being rejected by someone that I don't have any attached emotions to (I use 'attached' here to remind you that our attachments and expectations are the ones that hurt us most), and that is possibly what helped me deal with being rejected. It also helped me to not to lose connect with the child in me. Did you know that there is a therapy called 'Rejection Therapy' which encourages you to do things similar to what I'm doing? it says the rule is: to be rejected daily by someone for at least 30 days without a break. This therapy has been designed for anyone who wants to boost and grow their confidence and overcome the fear of being rejected. It is growth via rejection. The therapy shows you that rejection can be exciting, and instructs that you must put yourselves in a situation in which you will be rejected. If you get a positive response, that doesn't count, you really need to get rejected. So, get creative, smile at everyone you see, and count how many people ignored or rejected you. Ask a stranger to tell you a secret (which I used to do when I was in prep school along with my friends). Ask someone to give you their favorite object without any expectation of you returning it. Ask someone to do something wild with you. Get creative. You must know that people often reject us not because there is anything wrong with us but just because they were simply not interested in what we were offering at that time. When you get rejected and feel that you are not enough, ask yourself: is it the absolute truth? Am I really sure that I'm not enough and that's why I got rejected or fired or neglected or cheated on? Is it for sure? Am I 100% positive? Chances are, you will find out that your answer is, "I don't know… what I don't know! Most probably it is not how it looks like." So go ahead and put yourself in uncomfortable situations and if people aren't laughing at you and calling you crazy, then I would say you are not stretching enough. We grow the most through the things that stretch us the most. Remember, what doesn't kill you, makes you stronger ;)

- ***What do you eat?*** What kind of food you eat? Every one of us has our own body and blood type. To make it simple and short, eat the food that suits your body and blood type, take good care of the miraculous temple that we call our body that carries you. Love it and nourish it so that it loves you and nourishes you back. What kind of conversations are you consuming? Do you gossip and judge or envy others? Do you have valuable conversations or are you just talking about what did the Kardashians wear? Or why Brad Pitt and Angelina Jolie got divorced? Who is in your life? What kind of friends do you have? What kind of music or TV shows or news do you watch and nourish your mind with? Do you have negative people in your life who only drain your energy and do not support your growth? Remember that it won't be enough to just eat healthy but also stay in the same toxic relationship or have the same useless circle around you, or stay in the same job that you don't like. It will be like eating a healthy breakfast, but eating junk food for the rest of the day. Protect your energy. In aviation, the safety instructions are: in case of an emergency, put on your oxygen mask *first* and then help others. You can't be blind and help another blind person to cross the road. It is time to move to the next level, so, level up. Life is very exciting, and your time is too valuable to waste it on things that don't contribute to your growth.

- ***Question yourself first.*** Follow your heart, it never fails you. In order for you to know what you want and what stops you from being happy, you have to first ask yourself all the questions needed and write them down. No one and nothing will make you happy if you have no clue about what makes YOU happy and what YOU want. Not what society wants, nor your family or friends. You need to be genuine with yourself. Here are some questions as a starting point for you:
  1. What do I want?
  2. How will I know I've got what I want?
  3. What will I want if I didn't have to be unhappy about not getting it?
  4. What would happen if I allow myself to be happy without getting what I want?
  5. What would it mean about me if I allowed myself to be happy without getting what I want? Or, what it would mean about me if I allowed myself to be happy whether I got what I wanted or not?
  6. What am I afraid would happen if I got what I want?

7. What would I want if I knew I couldn't fail?
8. What would I want if I knew that it was OK to "fail"?
9. What would I want if I were certain to get it?
10. How do I make sense of the idea that I am already getting exactly what I want, that what I am getting in the moment is actually what I want?
11. If there was a miracle tonight, and when I woke up the next day, everything was exactly as I want it to be, how would I know a miracle had happened? What would I feel, what would I see, what would I hear, what would I believe, and what would I experience that would allow me to notice that a miracle had taken a place?

Most people don't allow themselves to acknowledge what they want, because of the fear of being unhappy if they don't get it. It is like the advertising myth that we need certain things to be happy, which leads to a lot of pressure for things to work (goals, success, material assets, etc.). Hence, it rarely works. Also, people sometimes think that being unhappy about having that specific thing will motivate them to take action towards it, instead of knowing that they are already built with an innate source of motivation and inspiration that they can trust fully and not need to use their unhappiness as a source of motivation. They have fears of the consequences of getting what they want. If a person wants to leave their job and start something they really love and while they are passionate about, but are afraid of "failure", then they will avoid losing their job and following their passion. If a person wants to lose weight, but they are afraid if they are going to cheat on their spouse, then they will avoid losing weight.

Core Values. Some questions, when asked and answered with the intention of being completely honest with yourself, will start eliciting your core values. Core values are the qualities that shape and describe your character and behavior and determine what you do, what you want, what you accept, and what you don't. Without them, you start to become imbalanced, distracted, disoriented, and not happy. Your core values are the solid ground of who you are. In order to make a decision in life, you need to make sure that it sits right with your core values, otherwise discomfort and self-doubt will start to arise. Some core values are: integrity, self-improvement, beauty, family, friendship, honesty, courage, discipline, fairness, respect, dignity, accountability, creativity, having fun, exercising, diversity, authenticity, trust, honor, faith, freedom, safety, etc. I would advise you to keep your core values in a short list that consists from three to ten core values so you can memorize them, as you will use them every day, throughout the day.

To help you shorten the list, define each value and know what it really means to you, you will need to ask yourself few questions for each value once the core values have been acknowledged. Some questions you could ask are:

- What will happen if I lose that specific value?
- Would I sacrifice any of these values for anything else like money?
- Have I lost any of these values in time of stress?
- Do I envision the rest of my life with that value?
- Will this change?
- Will I stop holding on to that value if it ever came to a competitive disadvantage to me at some point?
- Once done, you will come up with what I call core support – your own core that holds you and guides you. And once you apply them into your daily life routine, it will become a habit and then you will be choosing easily what sits right and resonates with who you are, starting from a meal decision to a career or a life partner, so choose carefully and wisely.

Law of Attraction. The beautiful thing about the law of attraction is that you can begin where you are and with nothing, and from nothingness, you can begin to generate within yourself the feelings of harmony, joy, and happiness. Only then will the law begin to respond to that good feeling. Start to have new beliefs, believe that there is more than enough in the Universe, that everything goes right for you, or that you are not getting older, you are getting wiser. You can create your life the way you want it by using the law of attraction. You can break yourself free from parents' rules, cultural codes, social beliefs, and prove once and for all that the power within you is greater than the power that's in the world that outside of you.

Most people will be thinking that is very nice, but *I* can't do that. I'm not strong enough to do that, or I'm not rich enough to do that, I'm not good enough to do that… and the list goes on…

Every single "I'm not" is only a creation. Your creation.

> *"Whether you think you can,*
> *or you can't either way you are right."*
>
> —*Henry Ford*

Call to Action. After doing the mental work, the physical work is now required. You can't close your eyes and wish for a flower to grow in your garden without planting a seed. It requires effort and, most importantly, it requires consistence. I had no clue when I started writing this book about where I was going to start, "how" I would publish it, who would publish it, or where I would sell it. Nothing at all. The only thing I knew was that I'm starting to write it, and I gave myself a certain amount of time to finish. I said everything else will work its way out for me; the Universe will arrange itself to give me what I need. And, in the middle of my writing, I received around three options to choose from. I trusted my intuition and here I am. The *how* will show up when the intention, commitment, and belief of the *why* and *what* are done. And if you feel the need for motivation and feel the need for support, reach out for help – with a friend or a trusted one, or by hiring a coach or a therapist who holds you accountable and supports you to achieve where you wish to be. And remember to celebrate every single achievement, no matter how small it is.

***

Meditation The goal of meditation is not to control your thoughts, but rather to stop letting them control you. In fact, one of the things we learn in the practice of meditation is not to worry about anything that crosses our mind, whether it's in the form of an image of us killing our boss or choking our mother-in-law, and simply treating it as a thought and let it pass like a cloud, without judging or rejecting it. It is the gateway to our unconscious mind through our awareness. Meditation activates alpha and theta brain waves – those brain waves are the ones activated while we are in a deep relaxation state, like the one before we fall asleep, or when we go sunbathing or have a hot bath. Here are few of the scientifically proven benefits of meditation:

1. **Reduces stress**. Many styles of meditation can help in reducing stress. Meditation can also help reduce symptoms in people with stress-triggered medical conditions.
2. Helps to **control anxiety**. Habitual meditation helps in reducing anxiety and anxiety-related mental health conditions like phobia, social anxiety, and OCD.
3. **Promotes emotional health.** Some forms of meditation can improve depression and optimize your outlook on life.
4. **Enhances self-awareness**. Different styles of meditation can help reconnect with yourself and know yourself better so you can make positive changes in your life.
5. **Increase attention span**. Many forms of meditation help in building your ability to redirect, shift, and maintain your attention.
6. **Helps reduce age-related memory loss**. The improvement of focus, attention, and clarity of thinking with regular meditation helps improve your memory.
7. **Generates kindness**. It develops positive, compassion, and loving feelings towards yourself and others.
8. **Helps in fighting addictions**. Meditation develops mental discipline and willpower and helps you avoid mental triggers for unwanted behaviors, helps in weight loss, get rid of unwanted habits, etc.
9. **Improves sleep**. Many techniques help in relaxing and controlling 'the monkey mind' as some monks may call it. They help shorten the time to sleep and improve sleep quality.

10. **Helps to control pain**. Meditation decreases the perception of pain in the mind.
11. **Decreases blood pressure**. Regular meditation decreases blood pressure and that could reduce strain around the heart and arteries and help to prevent heart disease.

The bottom line here is that meditation is both vital and very accessible. If you are someone who says that "Meditation is not my thing", or "I can't focus", or "I get irritated and distracted", or "My smallest toe feels uncomfortable" – any excuse you come up with after all the information that you have by now won't make any sense even to you.

The good news is that anyone can meditate and you can do so anywhere and at no cost. Know now that it is fine to be distracted; it is fine to think, "That is what your brain does throughout your whole life". In time, you will start to recognize your thoughts and shift your awareness.

You can't go to the gym once a week and expect a six pack. Your mind, as your body, as your soul, needs time to create a new habit. For some it takes few weeks, others a few months, and for still others, even a few years to master the mind. I have been meditating daily for over three years now and my mind still wanders around.

Begin with ten minutes a day with a very simple technique to start with.
- Sit upright with your spine erect.
- Take a deep breath in through the nose and then close your eyes.
- Hold your breath for a moment and then slowly exhale through the mouth.
- Become aware of your chest rising, pay attention to your body by focusing on the rising and falling of the chest and abdomen so it becomes your point of focus while meditating.
- Now, open your eyes and slowly take another deep breath and become aware of your surroundings. The sounds, the smell, the sights, the feelings.
- Do this for 10 minutes.

And if you are one of those who claim to not to have 10 minutes a day, then I will ask you if you even have a life! For those who did it and are willing to continue, thank you for taking a fully conscious breath through and within the present moment, the only moment that we have and that will ever exist.

- ***Journaling*** Researchers have found that writing about what you are grateful for, instead of just thinking about these things or typing them, is linked and wired with the brain to create new neuron connections, have better sleep, lower anxiety levels and improve the mood. Journaling is an opportunity for self-inquiry and discovery. It is simply just you, your thoughts, your feelings, a pen, and a notebook. There is so much potential in this simple act, you are giving yourself the permission to be present with yourself, open up your senses and listen to the whispers from within. Writing things down enables them to be processed. Old emotions are given acknowledgment and can then be released to give a room to new beliefs and manifestations. Journaling also sharpens your power of observation so that you can live each and every day with increased awareness of your connections with yourself, others and the world around you. And once you start noticing the details of life, it is like a flower that blossoms.

So, start your day with five minutes of journaling:
- Write down how you feel, scan your body, feel and see what your body is telling you and jot it down.
- Write down what is the question arising today?
  - What touches your soul?
  - What would your heart say?
  - When are you comfortable in your skin?
  - Where are your boundaries?
  - Where do you feel strong?

- How grateful you are just for the cup of tea you have, the new day you have, the freedom, safety, the sense of taste, touch, sound, smell, that you can speak of what you see?
- Why are you here?
- What are you afraid of?
- What does happiness feel like to you?
- What makes you feel connected?
- What or who do you need to forgive?
- What is getting in the way?
- If money were no object, what would you do?
- What is your story?
- What is the pay-off for not changing?
- If you would like to express gratitude for the new day, for the roof over your head, etc., what or whom do you want to say thank you for?
- What does kindness mean to you?
- How can you be kind to yourself?
- How can you develop your kindness toward others?
- What do you need to let go of?
- What do you want to know or learn today?
- What do you want to do today?

Journaling is a powerful way to start changing your reality.

> *"Whatever the mind can conceive and believe, the mind can achieve."*
>
> —*Napoleon Hill*

- **Visualizing** *Imagination is more important than knowledge.* That's what we do all the time, imagine. Our brain works with images and patterns. Remember? And, we associate feelings to these images and that is how our thoughts hurt us, because of the feeling that we associate with them. Remember that you are *feeling* your thoughts. The practice of visualization is extremely powerful. You can practice visualizing techniques for changing your reality, negative self-image, and eliminating negative self-talk. All you have to do is just literally allow your imagination to work for you. It is that simple. This process is deeply productive for bringing positivity to your mind, body, and spirit. It opens and expands your creative ability. It has been proven beyond doubt that visualization and meditation bring positive results to the practitioner. There is nothing that has been created without first having imagined it. Let me give you an example: "Don't think of the moon." We have to think of something in order to not to think about it, right? As another example, they had to visualize a car in order to build it. The one thing that will make your dreams come true is to *feel*. The passion that you add to the scenario or the thing you want, is the main drive and fuel for your vision. Feel that it is already yours, that it is here, and with the gratitude of your present moment and meditation, you are going to be able to do wonders.

- Start with something small. Hold an image of an old friend that you want to get in touch with and imagine that meeting or that phone call. Or imagine your favorite meal. There are so many things that we imagine all day long; pick something.
- Dwell only on the result and the outcome.
- Take a deep breath slowly, hold it for a moment and then exhale. Do this for couple of minutes to bring your awareness and attention to the present moment.
- Now start to visualize your scenario.
- Be patient with yourself, remember that everything takes time. When your mind goes somewhere else don't give up, bring it back to the moment with ease and enjoy the ride.

Remember that you are capable of more than you think you are, because you are more than you think you are. You are not your reality, you are not your name, you are not your nationality, you are not your body, you are an infinite, joyous, creative expression of life, with limitless potential, experiencing life through a physical form called a 'human being'. Your intuition and passion are your guide to what is possible for you.

There are many techniques associated with visualizing that I use with clients in order to help them change their lives. I will share a couple of them here that is so easy, and you can use it on your own.

1. <u>PHURBA TECHNIQUE:</u>
   This is a very powerful technique, to be used with great respect and care. This ancient technique is very effective and profound in changing one's neurology. It is a combination of visualization and an extremely powerful metaphor that can, and most often does, cause profound changes for people who use this exercise. It could be used for anything that you want to overcome or get rid of from your current and future experience in life. Whether it is a limiting belief or a physical pain, disease, etc., you pick your own ride. Sometimes it could take few weeks for major conditions; however, other problems could simply disappear without even a trace, right away. Use the exercise for one problem at a time.
   <u>Steps:</u>
   1. Get in touch mentally with the thought of having the problem or the specific condition, or even in the decision that been created in the first place.
   2. As you are mentally in touch with that thought, notice where in the body it represents itself physically or energetically and focus on that for just a moment.
   3. Mentally visualize pulling that energetic being (whatever symbolic representation you may imagine) out of

your body completely and fully. As you take it out of the body in front of you (this alone could be a very powerful experience for you physically), allow it, mentally, to show up in any shape or form in front of you, just outside of you. As it takes its shape, make sure that *all* of it is outside of your body; make sure that your body is clean of it and completely free.

4. Now, imagine holding in your hand any kind of knife, sword, or whatever your imagination finds appropriate for use in the following act. Imagine using your arm that is holding such an item in your hands and, literally in your mind, cut through this being, object, or entity. Cut through these boundaries and visualize it leaking out of itself and disappearing for good. Make sure that it has totally gone, completely disappeared.

5. Now repeat to yourself the thought that you would rather have instead. Make sure that you use positive language and only say and think of what you want (not what you don't want). As you now have the new empowering and desired thought, allow it to integrate in your neurology and embody it, lock it inside so that it stays there.

6. Speak out your gratitude. Be thankful and appreciate the powerful gift of being a human that you were given. The ability to change and resolve anything within your mind and your body is spectacular.

2. HO'OPONOPONO TECHNIQUE

Another ancient technique by the Hawaiians, it is mostly used for reconciliation and forgiveness. The English translation is simply 'correction'. It may sound too easy; however, it is recognized for its true power and potential in assisting you in your desired journey of life. The theory is aligned with what we learned earlier about repetitive patterns – that with the same common and pattern of knowledge in life, we keep repeating the same mistakes until we *truly* learn our lessons. And that only when we get the lesson do we stop repeating the same mistakes. That theory takes you to a level of awareness that allows you to realize that all your problems (and the good things in life) are just data. Data that keeps replaying in your mind like a broken record until you learn what needs to be learnt and clean it up. Once it's been cleaned up, it will be gone and it will stop showing in your life as you stop repeating the same mistake. The theory further suggests (also what we learned earlier) that the whole world outside of us is a reflection of what is inside of us. By now, we should be able to recognize the data (the problem) for what it truly is and do the following exercise to resolve it. The exercise is excellent to be used for any personal relationships, with anyone in your life, in any context. The good news is that much like the Phurba Technique, it can be equally effective not only for forgiveness or personal relationships, but for any other problem currently presenting itself in your life.

Say out loud and feel the meaning behind these words: ***I'm Sorry, I Love You, Please Forgive Me, Thank You.***

Keep repeating the above step until the issue is gone in your perception.

Step 1: Repentance – I'M SORRY

The phrase "I'm sorry" is usually painful to be said especially when we see the problem is 'out there'. This step holds you responsible for everything happening in your own mind. At first, you will most likely resist the idea of accepting to be responsible for 'out there'-type of problems. Once you realize that painful reality, it will then seem very natural to feel sorry by keep practicing the method more on your 'in here' problems and see results.

You can start with something you already reached a conclusion that you were responsible for causing it for yourself. For example, smoking, drugs, addictions, being over-weight, bad eating habits, etc. Do you have health issues? Anger or temper issues? Start with these issues that you have realized your responsibility towards and say you're sorry.

This is the whole point of this step. It is to realize that, "I am responsible for causing this (the issue) in my life and I feel terribly remorseful that something in my consciousness has caused that to happen."

Step 2: Love – I LOVE YOU
   Say I LOVE YOU, to yourself, your body, others, God, the Universe, nature, or whoever you believe in. Say I LOVE YOU to your challenges. Say it over and over. Mean it. Feel it. There is nothing more powerful than the power of Love.

Step 3: Ask Forgiveness – PLEASE FORGIVE ME
   Don't worry about who you're asking for forgiveness. Just ask! PLEASE FORGIVE ME. Say it over and over. Mean it. Remember your remorse from step 1 as you ask to be forgiven.

Step 4: Gratitude – THANK YOU
   Again, it doesn't matter who or what are you thankful for. Just say THANK YOU. Mean it and feel it. Thank yourself for doing the best you can with the knowledge and tools you have. Thank God, the Universe, the Divine, your mind. Thank people for being in your life. Thank people who left your life to leave space for the new to come in. Thank whatever and whoever was that just forgave you, and keep saying THANK YOU.

***

My To Do List By changing the blueprint of our inner reality, the outer reality will change. I would like to share with you my daily rituals. Please don't hesitate to take whatever feels comfortable from these rituals.

1. I wake up early (between 5.45-6.30 a.m.).
2. I open the curtains and look at the sky, pray/meditate to God, Universe, higher self, anything you believe in. I say, "Thank you for reviving me back to life so I can live another day." Then, I say the Christian Serenity prayer which is one of my favorite prayers: "God, grant me the serenity to accept the things I cannot change, the courage to change the things I can, and the wisdom to know the difference."
3. Do some breathing and meditation. You could choose to follow the 'brain and heart coherent' that I learned from my trainer Robert Simic (breathe in through the nose slowly for about five seconds, hold it for a moment, then breathe out equally slowly through the mouth, and repeat it for at least 5 minutes), do the Wim Hof breathing technique, or any other breathing technique you feel comfortable doing.
4. Then I spend some time visualizing.
5. I begin journaling, jot down what I'm grateful for, positive affirmations, what I feel, what I have achieved from my plans, etc.
6. I follow that up with yoga for 20-30 minutes.
7. Then I work out for 20-30 minutes.
8. And then I dance for at least 10 minutes.

9. Then I shower following the Wim Hof cold shower method.
10. I make an amazing morning smoothie for breakfast (spinach, kale, cucumber, fresh ginger, pear, mixed berries, fresh lemongrass, avocado) or whatever fruits and vegetables I fancy that day.

Once done, I start my day and run my errands. These rituals take me 2-3 hours every day, however, you don't have to do exactly the same especially when you are tight with time and schedule, or kids and family. You can start with 5 minutes journaling, 10 minutes breathing, a couple of minutes visualizing, 20-30 minutes exercise; and that will be perfect. Or even if you just start with 5 minutes breathing, it still will be perfect. The point is, start somewhere and one thing will lead to another. I started with 10 minutes meditation at the beginning, and look at what it's blossomed into! If you feel the need for motivation, look for a coach or therapist who lives near you or someone who has been recommended who can hold you accountable. As long as you start, you will be already on your journey to the inside of you.

You are who you've been looking for
So stop looking for more unless you are looking in a mirror
Because it is about time for you to see clearly that
You *are who you've been looking for.*

And that empty feeling you got,
That hole in your chest,
You only got that feeling because you think you are not blessed
With everything you need.
You see we live in a consumerist society
Which means they need you to buy stuff
And the easiest way to see it is to tell you
"You are not enough."

Buy this car, you'll get girls.
Buy this bra, you'll get guys.
And we are seeing it so much that we start believing these lies.
But the truth is:
The makeup they are selling to make you feel prettier
Is the same makeup you buy to stop feeling shittier
About this lie
They keep telling you
That "You are not enough"

And what about the movies we watch or the shows on TV
The more I watch the more I see
"I need you to complete me."

And yes, love is the answer, love is the key
But if you can't love yourself
How could you ever love me.

And loving yourself what does that even mean
Like massages and selfies and that sort of thing?
Because the more I think about it the more it feels weird
I've always been taught that self-love is something to be feared.

I've been taught that arrogance is bad
And vanity, it's not good.
And even my bracelets are telling me to act how Jesus would.
So, what should I do?
How should I act?
I am supposed to love myself.
But how do I even do that?

Well, I got a trick that I picked up from a friend.
Who noticed that I was quick to defend
Her
When she would say something negative about herself.
She would say "I am so dumb"
And I would say "You are so brilliant".
She would say "I am so weak"
And I would say "You are so resilient".
And when she said "I feel ugly"
And I said "You look beautiful,"
She asked me why I was so dutiful
Filling up her cup constantly
And yet treating my own cup so irresponsibly.

*Because when I looked in the mirror my voice was quite clear
"You are ugly, you are too thin,
Your hairline's receding, you got a pimple on your chin."
And that was when
She gave a piece of advice that changed my life:
She gave me a hug and she said,
"Treat yourself like someone you loved."*

*Treat yourself like someone you loved.
Now I've been standing, but I needed to be sitting
Because I couldn't believe that I've been letting
Myself keep forgetting
That I was who I've been looking for.
And deep in my core I knew it was time to stop looking for more
Until I could look through on my fear
And look into a mirror and see clearly
That the man looking back at me
Was the only one who can make me happy
And I AM ALREADY ENOUGH.*

*And I am not anymore special or unique than you
That is why I am here to speak to you
"YOU ARE ALREADY ENOUGH."
And when you start to see that you will start to be that
Your world will get brighter, your load will be lighter
And you can see that with life you can be a lover not a fighter*

And that life…
You deserve it.
Because you are worth it.
And there is no point in letting
Yourself keep forgetting because no matter
What you say or do":
"YOU ARE PERFECT."

And so, today I hope I leave you with a direction correction
Away from the flaws you see in your reflection.
They aren't flaws to me they are simply protection
Against all the doubts you have of your perfection.

So, start today.

Take a good long look in the mirror and say;
"I am who I've been looking for."

—*Adam Roa*

Forgiveness This process is mainly for you, for your beautiful self, not because the people who hurt you in any way deserve forgiveness. Nor is it about letting them back into your life, regardless of which role they were playing. Just because someone left you or hurt you in any form or caused you any pain does not mean they are bad human beings. Just because it ended does not mean they are unworthy of your love. That would be selfish thinking. To eliminate the selfish feelings and negative thoughts in your mind, you need to replace them with kindness and forgiveness.

You chose this person to stay in your life for a certain period of time, you never owned them, and it means that you found positive and convincing reasons to stay from the beginning. So, whether their soul left their bodies, or they left you to be with someone else, or to go somewhere else, don't put the blame on them and say they are bad people. Don't deny the happy moments and the laughter you had with them, don't deny the beautiful valuable time you spent together, don't deny the love and care you once had to each other, it was real, otherwise you wouldn't feel it to the core of your bones, but also, don't dwell on the past. Rather, say: "Thank you for allowing me to grow through this separation, thank you for leaving a room for whatever is coming next."

Remember this – no one is leaving this life alive, so live it as you would wish to live it. *You* are responsible and in control; no-one and nothing else can ever have control over you unless you allow them to.

A Message to Parents, ex-, Friend, Boss, or whoever you feel needs this message to be delivered to:

I would say send this message to the Universe and it will reach out.

I thank you for once being in my life, I thank you for once loving me and accepting me as I am. I appreciate the time and feelings we once had together. I don't look down on you; I love you and respect you the way you are and for who you were when I knew you. I forgive you for not being who I wanted you to be. I unconditionally love you and let you go.

Miss Corona!
I know you are out there somewhere, hiding in a corner feeding yourself from the fear in people's minds and hearts. You won't take too long from my precious time to write about you! I do acknowledge your existence as you affected the entire world, yes. However, this world widely impacts whether the impact is negative or positive. I will be talking about myself. I would rather think and focus on what I want and you are definitely not one of these things. So I choose to not focus on you. I also thank you for giving me the time to reflect on myself and having the least amount of distractions from the outer world! I know that this was not your intention, but, "Sorry, not sorry," babe. Too late! I already decided to take the most positive thing out of your impact. Thank you for giving me the time to write my first book, reflect on myself and my flaws and change what was needed to change, and carry on with my healing process and discover possibilities that I didn't know I have.

Because I choose who I want to be, and I choose to be healthy and happy.

CONCLUSION & CLOSURE

"Be at peace, so be it."

—Louise Hay.

As I promised myself to write my first book before my 30th birthday, I have written this book within six weeks. Not long after I turned 30, I left Dubai and moved back to Egypt for three months and was traveling locally. It was a completely different experience for me. Despite the country's flaws, Egypt has treated me so well. I attracted totally different events, circumstances, and people. Even those who I knew long ago – their behavior has changed. That was a living experience for me which proved that once we change our internal world, the outer one changes accordingly.

I then moved to Bali, Indonesia, or the Island of Gods, as they call it. Learning, expanding, growing, and evolving greatly on a daily basis, discovering even more knowledge. This journey is showing me where I need to heal and let go, attracting so many events, challenges, and people that present to me my strengths and weaknesses. That has led to a whole new book that I'm writing and will be sharing with you soon.

Hope you enjoyed your journey with me during this book and see you in another adventure.

ABOUT THE AUTHOR

A world traveler with Egyptian roots, Mahi Amin is a certified NLP practitioner, hypnotist, time paradigm techniques practitioner, and Transformational Life-Coach with over 11 years of experience in many and varied fields that she draws from as she coaches her clients. Throughout her careers, she has helped a number of people across different age groups all over the world.

Mahi makes use of broad life experiences and knowledge to fulfill her passion of helping people reset their emotional, mental, and physical well-being to live the life of their dreams.

If you would like to get in touch with me or work with me one-on-one, you can use any of the following links. I hope to connect with you in person.

Website: www.mahiamin.com
Email: ma@mahiamin.com
YouTube: Mahi Amin
Facebook: Itsmahiamin
Instagram: Its.mahiamin

www.ingramcontent.com/pod-product-compliance
Lightning Source LLC
Chambersburg PA
CBHW020905080526
44589CB00011B/458